$p g^s$ 16
100
101

"Illegal But Not Criminal"

John E. Conklin is Associate Professor of Sociology at Tufts University. He is the author of *Robbery and the Criminal Justice System* and *The Impact of Crime* and editor of *The Crime Establishment* (Prentice-Hall). Professor Conklin has also published many papers in scholarly journals.

John E. Conklin

"Illegal But Not Criminal"

Business Crime in America

A SPECTRUM BOOK

PRENTICE-HALL, INC., Englewood Cliffs, New Jersey 07632

Library of Congress Cataloging in Publication Data

CONKLIN, JOHN E
  "Illegal but not criminal."

    (A Spectrum Book)
    Includes bibliographical references and index.
    1. Commercial crimes—United States. 2. Corporations
    —United States—Corrupt practice. 3. White collar
    crimes—United States. I. Title.
HV6769.C65   364.1'6   77-7621
ISBN 0-13-450890-4
ISBN 0-13-450882-3 pbk.

© 1977 by Prentice-Hall, Inc.
Englewood Cliffs, New Jersey 07632

A SPECTRUM BOOK

10   9   8   7   6   5   4   3   2

Printed in the United States of America

PRENTICE-HALL INTERNATIONAL, INC., *London*
PRENTICE-HALL OF AUSTRALIA PTY. LIMITED, *Sydney*
PRENTICE-HALL OF CANADA, LTD., *Toronto*
PRENTICE-HALL OF INDIA PRIVATE LIMITED, *New Delhi*
PRENTICE-HALL OF JAPAN, INC., *Tokyo*
PRENTICE-HALL OF SOUTHEAST ASIA PTE. LTD., *Singapore*
WHITEHALL BOOKS LIMITED, *Wellington, New Zealand*

For Chris and Annie

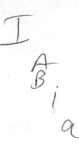

Contents

Preface, xi

Acknowledgments, xiii

one
The Legitimate Rackets   **1**

The Costs of Business Crime, 2
The Study of Business Crime, 8

two
Business Crime and the Public   **16**

Studies of Public Opinion toward Business Crime, 20
Studies of Public Opinion toward Employee Theft, 27

three
Business Crime and the Economy   **34**

The Consumption-Oriented Economy, 34
Competition and Profit, 41
The Market Structure, 51

Trust.and Credit, 56
The Corporate Structure, 64

four
The Psychology and Sociology of Business Crime   **72**

Psychological Explanations of Business Crime, 74
Learning Business Crime, 78
Justifying Business Crime, 86

five
Business Crime and the Criminal Justice System   **100**

Prosecution and Sentencing of Business Offenders, 100
Reasons for Leniency toward Business Offenders, 109

six
Reducing Crime in the Business World   **130**

The Creation of a Countervailing Force, 130
Reforming the Criminal Justice System, 135

Index, 149

Preface

During the last few years there has been increased attention given to the problem of crime in the business world. Except for a few radical critiques of capitalism, though, there has been little effort by sociologists to examine this problem. This book tries to fill that gap by examining the existing literature on violations of the law by businessmen and corporations and by developing a framework within which to investigate business crime. Although no original data are presented in this book, it is hoped that the synthesis of existing material—much of which has been ignored by sociologists—will provide a basis for future research studies. In presenting this material, we have tried to avoid both a blanket condemnation and defense of all business behavior; instead, we look at one specific type of business behavior, that which violates the law.

Acknowledgments

I am grateful to the late Erwin O. Smigel for originally stimulating my interest in business crime. We collaborated on a paper, "Norms and Attitudes toward Business-Related Crimes," which we presented in March 1972 at the Symposium on Studies of Public Experience, Knowledge and Opinion of Crime and Justice, sponsored by the Bureau of Social Science Research, Inc., in Washington D.C. I have drawn on that paper in Chapters 2 and 4. I would also like to express appreciation for the assistance provided by Joseph Fisher, David Kovacs, and Jane Milner.

The chart on pages 48 and 49 is reprinted by permission of *Newsweek*.

The chart on page 126 — © 1975 by The New York Times Company — is reprinted by permission.

The excerpt from *The Billion Dollar Sure Thing* by Paul E. Erdman (New York: Charles Scribner's Sons, 1973) is used by permission of Charles Scribner's Sons and Hutchinson Publishing Group Ltd. The British title for this work is *The Billion Dollar Killing*.

one

The
Legitimate Rackets

An executive of an electrical equipment manufacturing company who was involved in a massive price-fixing conspiracy was asked by a congressional committee's attorney if he knew that his meetings with his co-conspirators were illegal. He replied: "Illegal? Yes, but not criminal. I didn't find that out until I read the indictment. . . . I assumed that criminal action meant damaging someone, and we did not do that."[1] Actually, that price-fixing conspiracy cost consumers millions of dollars. The fact that considerable damage was indeed done is reflected in the imprisonment of a number of the executives who were involved, in the imposition of $1.8 million in fines on the companies, and in the awarding of over $160 million in civil damages to plaintiffs against one of the companies.

The picture of white collar crime as illegal but not criminal is reinforced by the mass media. "The crime problem" is dealt with in sensationalized front-page stories which tell of murder, rape, and robbery. When business crimes such as price-fixing and food adulteration are dealt with, they are most commonly reported in the business pages. When a millionaire proposes a Christmas airlift to American troops in South Vietnam, the story makes national headlines; when the same man is

---

[1]Cited in Gilbert Geis, "White Collar Crime: The Heavy Electrical Equipment Antitrust Cases of 1961," in *Criminal Behavior Systems: A Typology*, ed. Marshall B. Clinard and Richard Quinney (New York: Holt, Rinehart and Winston, Inc., 1967), p. 144.

1

sued for $90 million for an alleged stock fraud a few years later, little is heard about the incident.[2] Although the media have paid increasing attention to white collar crime in the last few years, they have rarely dealt with it as part of "the crime problem."

The reporting of official statistics on crime also influences the way in which crime is perceived in the United States. The Federal Bureau of Investigation issues regular reports on crimes which are reported to the police. Much attention is given to the "index crimes" of murder, rape, robbery, aggravated assault, burglary, larceny, and auto theft. Less information is provided for 22 other crimes; included among these are three offenses which are sometimes committed by businessmen—embezzlement, fraud, and arson. Because few business crimes are reported to the police, little can be learned of them from FBI statistics. Although some information on white collar crime is available in the annual reports of federal regulatory agencies, it is not reported at regular press conferences nor summarized on the front pages of the newspapers.

The Costs of Business Crime

The costs of business crime are pervasive and exorbitant. As one judge said, "In our complex society the accountant's certificate and the lawyer's opinion can be instruments for inflicting pecuniary loss more potent than the chisel or the crowbar."[3] However, the economic costs of business crime are often difficult to assess, as can be seen from the following example:

> If a buyer for an automobile manufacturer takes a $25,000 bribe from a supplier of shock absorbers in connection with a $1 million contract, what is the true social and economic cost? It is not the $25,000. It is not the difference between the contract price and what someone else would have charged (such differential might be small). The true loss might be measured in these ways, of course, or by a qualitative evaluation of the shock absorbers supplied, but the major loss might well be the erosion of

[2]Jon Nordheimer, "Texan Says He'll Send Families of Prisoners to Paris for Plea," *The New York Times,* December 20, 1969, p. 15; Robert J. Cole, "$90-Million Fraud Suit Filed Here against Perot," *The New York Times,* July 2, 1975, pp. 45, 47.

[3]Cited in Robert M. Morgenthau, "Equal Justice and the Problem of White Collar Crime," *Conference Board Record,* 6 (August 1969), 17.

the integrity of the buying operation itself which could contribute to further losses in other transactions.[4]

Some business crime may even be "victimless" because no apparent harm is suffered by either party to the crime and because neither party wishes to make a formal complaint about the violation. For example, a construction firm might make a payoff to obtain a permit to move machinery across a city sidewalk. In such a case, neither the construction company nor the city agency would think of itself as victimized and neither would make a formal complaint. However, the owner of the building would pay for the bribe in the final price of the building. If the owner knows of the bribe and considers it a legitimate part of the cost of building construction, he would not consider himself a victim. However, the owner might choose to recover the cost of the payoff through slightly increased rents for the tenants of the building. In such a case, the tenants would suffer a real loss, although they would probably never know that their rent included the cost of a bribe.

Another type of business crime which might appear to be victimless is an illegal campaign contribution by a corporation. One could argue that this act undermines the strength of the government; however, this argument may not be much stronger than is the reasoning that such "victimless" crimes as gambling and homosexuality undermine the morality of the nation and should thus be punished as criminal behavior. When a corporation makes an illegal contribution to a political candidate, neither considers itself a victim and neither makes a formal complaint. However, corporate campaign contributions are often concealed from stockholders and may result in diminished dividends for them. If such payments were known to and approved by stockholders, one could argue that they were not victims; it would then be difficult to specify any individual or institution which suffered direct harm from the illegal contribution.[5]

Most business crimes involve an obvious victim: a defrauded stockholder, a deceived customer, or a company which has lost money through

---

[4]Herbert Edelhertz, *The Nature, Impact and Prosecution of White-Collar Crime* (Washington, D.C.: U.S. Government Printing Office, 1970), pp. 8-9.

[5]That stockholders sometimes support corporate payoffs was suggested by the warm reception that stockholders gave to one corporate chairman who had recently pleaded guilty to illegal campaign contributions, and by an overwhelming vote by another company's stockholders against laws which would have prohibited their company from making illegal payoffs. See Louis M. Kohlmeier, "The Bribe Busters," *The New York Times Magazine*, September 26, 1976, p. 60.

employee theft. The direct cost of business crime surpasses the cost of such conventional crimes as larceny, robbery, burglary, and auto theft. In 1965 the estimated loss from these four crimes was about $600 million;[6] with inflation and rising crime rates, a better estimate as of 1977 would be about $3 to $4 billion per year. This figure pales in significance when compared with an estimated annual loss of $40 billion from various white collar crimes.[7] Half that amount results from consumer fraud, illegal competition, and deceptive practices. A different estimate places the cost of wasteful car repairs at $9 billion a year and the cost of deceptive grocery labeling at $14 billion a year.[8]

Almost $4 billion a year is lost in securities thefts and frauds. Financial fraud is costly to all types of investors, from middle-income families who have a lifetime's savings wiped out to large institutions which have to reduce dividends to investors because of their own investment losses. The taxpaying public also loses in such frauds because financial losses are often tax-deductible, meaning that others must make up lost revenue through higher taxes or else suffer curtailed government services.[9]

The large losses from such business crimes as stock fraud may increase in the future with the acceleration in the use of computer technology. Although the introduction of computers may reduce certain types of theft, because many people lack the skills to operate computers, it will also increase the opportunity for very costly crimes. A study of twelve cases of bank embezzlement by computer found an average loss of $1,090,000.[10] During the early 1970s the total annual loss from computer crimes (excluding the $2 billion loss in the Equity Funding case) averaged about $10 or $15 million.[11]

Consumers suffer a financial loss from noncompetitive market situations, some of which are due to antitrust violations. Not all noncompeti-

---

[6]The President's Commission on Law Enforcement and Administration of Justice, *Task Force Report: Crime and Its Impact—An Assessment* (Washington, D.C.: U.S. Government Printing Office, 1967), p. 42.

[7]Chamber of Commerce of the United States, *A Handbook on White Collar Crime* (Washington, D.C.: Chamber of Commerce of the United States, 1974), p. 6.

[8]Senator Philip A. Hart, as cited in Charles H. McCaghy, *Deviant Behavior: Crime, Conflict, and Interest Groups* (New York: Macmillan Publishing Co., Inc., 1976), p. 205.

[9]Donald Moffitt, "Introduction," in *Swindled: Classic Business Frauds of the Seventies,* ed. Donald Moffitt (Princeton, N.J.: Dow Jones Books, 1976), p. vii.

[10]W. Thomas Porter, Jr., "Computer Raped by Telephone," *The New York Times Magazine,* September 8, 1974, p. 40.

[11]Donn B. Parker, *Crime by Computer* (New York: Charles Scribner's Sons, 1976), p. 28.

tive situations are the result of violation of the law; for instance, fair trade laws, a guaranteed legal monopoly which has only recently been eliminated, cost consumers as much as $2 billion a year in recent years.[12] The noncompetitive state of the auto industry may cost consumers as much as $16 billion a year.[13] Lack of competition in the pharmaceutical industry costs consumers millions of dollars each year. Introducing competition would often reduce prices; in 1964, antitrust action against the manufacturers of the drug tetracycline reduced its price by 75 percent.[14] An order by the Securities and Exchange Commission which forced stockbrokers to stop fixing their fees and to compete with each other resulted in a saving to stock purchasers of an estimated $25 million in the first month alone.[15]

Violations of the law by businessmen not only cost money; they may also lead to physical harm or even death. Death by botulism poisoning from contaminated vichyssoise in 1972 apparently resulted from unsanitary plant conditions and inadequate government inspections. Some investigators believe that the death in a 1974 car crash of Karen Silkwood, a nuclear power plant worker, was a murder designed to curtail her leaking information to the press regarding plant hazards and company falsification of inspection records. In 1976 the General Accounting Office reported that over the previous decade 54 persons had died of blood poisoning and 410 had been injured as a result of the use of contaminated intravenous drugs. Although such serious injuries and deaths as occurred in these cases are often unintentional and inadvertent, the acts of omission and negligence which produce those results are sometimes criminal.

Violations of the law by businessmen may involve the corruption of government officials and the subversion of the public interest. Illegal campaign contributions provide wealthy corporations with political influence which is hidden from public view and which weakens the democratic process. Bribes paid by American corporations to political parties and influential individuals abroad often constitute interference

[12]Eileen Shanahan, " 'Fair Trade' Laws Repealed by U.S.," *The New York Times*, December 13, 1975, p. 1.

[13]Mark J. Green, with Beverly C. Moore, Jr., and Bruce Wasserstein, *The Closed Enterprise System* (New York: Grossman Publishers, 1972), p. 4.

[14]"More Punch for Antitrust—Moves You Can Expect," *U. S. News & World Report*, 77 (November 25, 1974), 47.

[15]"Brokers Say Rate War Cost $25-Million in May," *The New York Times*, September 11, 1975, pp. 35, 39.

with the government of those nations and may be harmful to American foreign policy. American corporations, sometimes in conjunction with the Central Intelligence Agency, have also engaged in the subversion and overthrow of democratically elected regimes which are seen as antagonistic to American business and political interests.

Crime in the business world does not always involve the corporation as the offender; often the corporation is the victim. Losses from employee theft and embezzlement weaken firms. The annual loss from employee theft and shoplifting is about $5 to $10 billion a year; between one-third and three-fourths of that amount is due to employee theft.[16] A 1974 estimate placed the annual loss from employee theft and embezzlement at $7 billion.[17] Sometimes the losses from such theft are chronic rather than sudden. For example, one department store cashier took one nickel, dime, or quarter from every roll of change she made over a period of twenty years; she was able to purchase a home with the money she stole.[18] When small amounts are multiplied over many years or over many workers, the losses are staggering. Using lie-detector tests with chain store employees in Chicago a number of years ago, one investigator found that 76 percent of them were taking money or merchandise.[19] The extensiveness of employee theft is also seen in the fact that Montgomery Ward in a recent year fired 3 percent of its work force (4,000 workers) for stealing a total of $2.5 million in merchandise; undoubtedly much more than that in losses went undiscovered.[20] Losses directly due to employee theft and the costs of insurance to protect against such thefts are usually passed on to consumers in higher prices; such costs may account for as much as 15 percent of all the money spent for goods and services in this country.[21]

Losses from employee theft and embezzlement cause as many as a thousand businesses to go bankrupt each year. One spokesman for the insurance industry suggests that as many as 30 percent of all business failures may be due to employee theft, although other estimates place

---

[16]McCaghy, *Deviant Behavior*, p. 178.

[17]U.S. Chamber of Commerce, *White Collar Crime*, p. 6.

[18]"Retailing: The Thieves Within," *Newsweek*, 86 (November 24, 1975), 103.

[19]J.P. McEvoy, "The Lie Detector Goes into Business," *Forbes*, January 15, 1941, p. 16.

[20]"Retailing," p. 107.

[21]Norman Jaspan, *Mind Your Own Business* (Englewood Cliffs, N.J.: Prentice-Hall, Inc., 1974), p. 201.

the proportion at half that figure.[22] During the 1950–71 period there were as many as one hundred bank failures which were directly attributable to fraud or embezzlement.[23] During the first half of 1975, commercial banks in the United States lost nearly five times as much money in frauds and embezzlements, usually by insiders, as they did from armed bank robberies.[24]

Businesses also suffer from antitrust violations by their competitors; such offenses weaken their competitive position in the marketplace and may even force them out of business. Advertising fraud by a competitor may reduce an honest firm's sales. Research espionage leading to the theft of ideas and designs may be costly to a company which pays the bill for research and then gains little in profits when its ideas are stolen. Industrial sabotage by workers or by outsiders results in the costly destruction of machinery and merchandise.

Even more significant than the financial and physical costs of white collar crime may be the destructive impact of such behavior on public confidence in the economy and the commercial world.[25] The President's Commission on Law Enforcement and Administration of Justice, which devoted little space in its seventeen published volumes to the topic of white collar crime, nevertheless states that such offenses "are the most threatening of all—not just because they are so expensive, but because of their corrosive effect on the moral standards by which American business is conducted."[26] Business crime undermines public faith in the economic system because such crime is integrated with "the structure of legitimate business."[27] Such crime reduces willingness to engage in commercial transactions. Stock manipulations and frauds undermine the capitalist system, which requires public investment for capital. The discovery of fraud through adulteration and mislabeling of grain which is shipped abroad has created distrust among foreign businessmen who

[22]"Crime Expense: Now Up to $51 Billion a Year," *U.S. News & World Report,* 69 (October 26, 1970), 33.

[23]McCaghy, *Deviant Behavior,* p. 178.

[24]"The Increase in Bank Thefts," *The New York Times,* October 19, 1975, p. 6.

[25]Edwin H. Sutherland, *White Collar Crime* (New York: Holt, Rinehart and Winston, 1949, 1961), p. 13.

[26]The President's Commission on Law Enforcement and Administration of Justice, *The Challenge of Crime in a Free Society* (Washington, D.C.: U.S. Government Printing Office, 1967), p. 5.

[27]Elmer Hubert Johnson, *Crime, Correction and Society,* 3rd ed. (Homewood, Ill.: The Dorsey Press, 1974), p. 163.

purchase grain from American companies. A director of a European corporation has said: "Our main concern is trying to get what we pay for. But you may not realize how important this is to the United States. You and your farmers are losing a major market. A lot of mistrust is building up."[28] Due to misgrading and adulteration, foreign buyers may shift their purchases to other nations. This would be more costly to American farmers than to the large grain corporations, which are often international in scope and would continue to profit even if foreign buyers turned to other suppliers.

Business crime also sets an example of disobedience for the general population. Crimes by the upper class, especially if they do not lead to conviction and imprisonment, serve as rationalizations for the lower classes to justify their own criminal behavior. Bitterness at class and racial discrimination in the criminal justice system also makes traditional offenders resistant to rehabilitation. Unpunished violations by white collar offenders create disrespect for the law and engender a desire for revenge against those who protect their own but punish society's outcasts. For example, consumer fraud and exploitation was one underlying cause of the frustrations which led to the riots in black ghettoes during the 1960s.

The Study of Business Crime

Scholarly interest in business crime has existed since the turn of the century, although most of the work on the subject has been done since the concept of white collar crime was introduced by sociologist Edwin H. Sutherland in a speech before the American Sociological Society in 1939. In 1907 sociologist E. A. Ross wrote about "criminaloids," men who engaged in "flagitious" practices which were sometimes in violation of the law. He said that these individuals acknowledged the approved social goals of monetary success and power, but that it was difficult to focus public attention on their crimes because they lacked "the brimstone smell."[29] In 1912 economist Thorstein Veblen compared the captain of industry with the juvenile delinquent in his "unscrupulous conversion of goods and persons to his own ends, and a callous disregard of the feel-

[28]William Robbins, "Europe Grain Men Press Complaints," *The New York Times,* June 6, 1975, pp. 1, 36.

[29]Edward Alsworth Ross, *Sin and Society: An Analysis of Latter-Day Iniquity* (Boston: Houghton Mifflin, 1907), p. 47.

ings and wishes of others, and of the remoter effects of his actions."[30] The muckraking tradition of the 1920s exposed the destructive impact of various capitalistic practices, leading to reforms which reduced but did not eliminate such problems as food adulteration and price-fixing. In 1934 sociologist Albert Morris argued for a shift in the emphasis of criminology from traditional crimes to offenses by those in positions of economic power.[31] He said that although they were often habitual offenders, the "criminals of the upperworld" were rarely punished by the criminal justice system or stigmatized by public condemnation.

In 1949, ten years after he introduced the notion of white collar crime, Sutherland published *White Collar Crime*. He defines the subject matter of the book "approximately as a crime committed by a person of respectability and high social status in the course of his occupation."[32] It is unclear what the term "respectability" means here, since Sutherland distinguishes it from "high social status"; it may mean that a white collar criminal is one who has not previously been convicted of a traditional crime or who does not think of himself as a criminal. The exact meaning of high social status is also unclear. Sutherland suggests that the term applies to those who are wealthy or who occupy positions of high prestige; however, he does not limit his analysis of white collar crime to people of high status, for he examines offenses by such workers as bank tellers and repairmen.[33]

Because of the respectability and high social status of white collar offenders, some scholars have suggested that such individuals are not really criminals at all. They claim that it is paradoxical that the leaders of a community could also be its criminals.[34] They say that although their behavior may violate the law in a "technical legal sense," they are

[30]Cited in Herbert A. Bloch and Gilbert Geis, *Man, Crime and Society,* 2nd ed. (New York: Random House, 1970), p. 304.

[31]Albert Morris, "Criminals of the Upperworld," in Albert Morris, *Criminology* (New York: Longmans, Green and Co., 1935), pp. 152-58.

[32]Sutherland, *White Collar Crime,* p. 9.

[33]Viewing white collar crime in terms of the respectability and social status of the offender creates confusion, because such a definition includes characteristics of individuals as well as a type of behavior. Crimes such as murder, rape, and robbery are not defined in terms of an offender's social status; these types of behavior are crimes irrespective of the perpetrator of the act. The failure to define white collar crime in terms unrelated to the characteristics of the offender has led some sociologists to argue for a concept of "occupational crime," violations of the law which are directly linked to a job. For example, see Marshall B. Clinard and Richard Quinney, *Criminal Behavior Systems: A Typology,* 2nd ed. (New York: Holt, Rinehart and Winston, Inc., 1973), pp. 187-205.

[34]George B. Vold, *Theoretical Criminology* (New York: Oxford University Press, 1958), pp. 253-55.

not real criminals because they do not see themselves as criminals and because they lack "the spiritual attitude . . . of the criminal."[35] However, there is no concrete evidence that businessmen who violate the law actually do maintain a noncriminal self-concept. Even if they do so, this would lead us not simply to accept as valid their assessment of themselves, but rather to ask *how* they maintain such a self-concept in the face of evidence to the contrary. To suggest that white collar crime should be defined by the attitudes of the perpetrators would logically imply that murderers and rapists should also be questioned about their attitudes toward the criminality of their acts. It is the law rather than the opinion of the offender which defines behavior as criminal or noncriminal.

Some of Sutherland's critics claim that the laws which businessmen violate are not criminal laws in the usual sense.[36] They argue that many white collar crimes are merely sharp practices which are consistent with the basic business ideology of profit and which rarely fall under the regular criminal code. This criticism does direct attention to the issue of the historical origin of the laws which regulate business, but it overlooks the fact that many of the laws are actually extensions of common-law concepts to problems which have emerged as the economy has changed. Even the rather suddenly imposed price controls under the Office of Price Administration (OPA) during and after World War II defined behavior as illegal which had a long tradition of being criminal, e.g., conspiracy against the government, tax evasion, fraud, and bribery.

Critics have also asserted that the laws which define white collar crimes are vague. Although some such laws are not clearly defined, most are quite specific as to which types of behavior will be treated as criminal. Some white collar crimes may be accidental violations, but more are intentional. The 1961 electrical equipment price-fixing conspiracy showed willful, blatant, and flagrant violations of the law.[37] Violations of the OPA regulations were "complex, evasive, and willful" and "legally, logically, and technically" criminal.[38]

Sutherland claims that criminal courts are not the only agencies

[35]Ernest W. Burgess, "Comment," *American Journal of Sociology*, 56 (July 1950), 32–34; Ross, *Sin and Society*, p. 48.

[36]Vold, *Theoretical Criminology*, p. 250; Walter C. Reckless, *The Crime Problem*, 5th ed. (New York: Appleton-Century-Crofts, 1973), p. 316.

[37]Geis, "White Collar Crime," p. 141.

[38]Marshall B. Clinard, *The Black Market: A Study of White Collar Crime* (Montclair, N.J.: Patterson Smith, 1952, 1969), p. viii; Frank E. Hartung, "White-Collar Offenses in the Wholesale Meat Industry in Detroit," "Rejoinder," *American Journal of Sociology*, 56 (July 1950), p. 26.

which make official decisions about violations of the criminal law; decisions by civil courts and by administrative agencies may also indicate criminal guilt. If such an agency finds that certain behavior has been engaged in which *could have* been sanctioned with a criminal penalty had the case been tried in criminal court, Sutherland calls the behavior white collar crime. Sutherland has been criticized for using punishability as the best criterion for defining crime; his critics prefer to limit the usage of the term "criminal" to persons who have been convicted beyond a reasonable doubt, in a criminal court, of an intentional violation of the law and who suffer a criminal sanction such as imprisonment, a fine, or probation.[39] Sutherland has also been attacked for confusing civil law, which is concerned with the reparation and distribution of economic losses among individuals, with criminal law, which is concerned with the punishment of morally culpable behavior. Although the civil law theoretically serves individual interests and the criminal law theoretically serves social interests, it is often difficult to make that distinction in practice. Also, differences between the administration of the civil law and the administration of the criminal law are often less in practice than in theory.[40] However, because civil courts and regulatory agencies do not apply the due process rights and procedural safeguards which criminal courts supposedly do, a decision by one of these agencies may be made on less evidence than would be required for a criminal conviction.

Sutherland's work freed criminology from total reliance on official crime statistics, which measure only a part of the crime problem. He also contributed to the sociology of law by directing attention to the way in which laws regulating business behavior are written and enforced.[41] Some critics feel that he acted more as a muckraker and propagandist than as a social scientist, seeking more to change public attitudes toward corporation crime than to revise the domain of criminology.[42] Others

[39]Paul W. Tappan, "Crime and the Criminal," *Federal Probation,* 11 (July-September 1947), 44; Robert G. Caldwell, "A Re-examination of the Concept of White-Collar Crime," *Federal Probation,* 22 (March 1958), 30-36.

[40]Harold E. Pepinsky, "From White Collar Crime to Exploitation: Redefinition of a Field,"*Journal of Criminal Law and Criminology,* 65 (June 1974), 225-33.

[41]Indeed, one student of white collar crime has said that more attention has been given to the origin of the laws regulating business than to the causes of the behavior which violates the law. Vilhelm Aubert, "White Collar Crime and Social Structure," *American Journal of Sociology,* 58 (November 1952), 263.

[42]Gilbert Geis, "Toward a Delineation of White Collar Offenses," *Sociological Inquiry,* 2 (Spring 1962), 160-71; Vold, *Theoretical Criminology,* pp. 243-61.

accept his assertion that he was seeking to expand the subject matter of modern criminology.[43] Whatever his motivation, Sutherland did produce an innovative and important study of a previously neglected type of law-violating behavior.

Relatively few empirical studies of white collar crime have been carried out since Sutherland's ground-breaking work. Sociological studies of crime in the business world have been done of imprisoned embezzlers (Cressey), violations of OPA regulations in the Detroit meat industry (Hartung), OPA violations during and after World War II (Clinard), tax evasion by landlords (Groves), rent control violations by landlords (Ball), and prescription violations by pharmacists (Quinney). Most other work has taken the form of investigative journalism and biographies of notorious business offenders. A number of articles on legal aspects of business crime have appeared in law journals, and business periodicals often contain articles on the subject. However, there has been no integrated and systematic sociological analysis of this material in recent years.

One reason for the absence of work on white collar crime is that few data are available on such offenses. Police reports are generally devoid of such information, and regulatory commission reports often lack detail and representativeness. Also missing are interviews, life histories, and autobiographies of businessmen, both those who have violated the law and those who have resisted the temptation to do so. There is also little information on the types of business organizations and market structures which are conducive to or resistant to business crime.

Another reason for the dearth of studies of business crime is that such behavior is often extraordinarily complex. The manipulations of business offenders are commonly intended to deceive other businessmen. If businessmen close to the offender cannot understand how they are being victimized, students of such behavior who must view it from a distance are at an even greater disadvantage in trying to comprehend the behavior. For example, Robert Vesco's looting of the Investors Overseas Services involved intricate maneuvers which even his closest business associates could not understand. An SEC complaint against him and 41 other defendants was 17,000 words long and took eight lawyers a total

---

[43]Seldon D. Bacon, "Review of Sutherland, *White Collar Crime*," *American Sociological Review*, 15 (April 1950), 309-10; Hermann Mannheim, *Comparative Criminology* (Boston: Houghton Mifflin Company, 1965), p. 472; Donald R. Cressey, "Foreword," in Sutherland, *White Collar Crime*, p. iii.

of twenty months to research and write.[44] Obviously, such an investigation is beyond the resources of scholarly investigators.

In this book we shall use the term "business crime" to limit our area of inquiry. *Business crime is an illegal act, punishable by a criminal sanction, which is committed by an individual or a corporation in the course of a legitimate occupation or pursuit in the industrial or commercial sector for the purpose of obtaining money or property, avoiding the payment of money or the loss of property, or obtaining business or personal advantage.*[45] This definition assumes a violation of an existing law; no attempt will be made to assess the morality of business behavior which does not violate a law. However, it includes behavior which violates a criminal law but which is not dealt with in a criminal court; behavior which is criminally punishable but is dealt with in civil court or by an administrative agency will be treated as business crime. We shall avoid referring to the perpetrators of such acts as criminals unless they are convicted and criminally sanctioned.

This definition is broader but less ambiguous than Sutherland's, since it does not limit the behavior to individuals of high social status and respectability. Employee theft and embezzlement by low-status personnel within a business organization can thus be examined. We retain Sutherland's emphasis on occupation, but depart from both his definition and from more recent definitions of occupational crime by avoiding analysis of crime by occupational groups not within the business or commercial sector of society. Thus we shall exclude from consideration such offenses as fee-splitting by physicians, ambulance-chasing by lawyers, extortion by politicians, medical quackery (which is primarily perpetrated by offenders engaged in crime on a full-time basis), and abuse of unemployment benefits (which is a crime by an unemployed person against the government).

One reason to limit the discussion to business crimes is that many of the elements of the commercial world which are conducive to business crime are absent in other occupational settings. In contrast to physicians and lawyers, businessmen on the whole seem to have less prestige in the eyes of the public. In Chapter 2, the nature of public opinion toward business offenders will be examined and the impact of that opinion on

[44]Alexander Cockburn, "Million Dollar Yeggs," *The New York Review of Books*, March 20, 1975, p. 21.

[45]This definition is an adaptation of the useful definition offered in Edelhertz, *Nature, Impact and Prosecution*, pp. 3–4.

business crime will be explored. A number of elements of the business world which are conducive to business crime—such as the heavy emphasis on profits, the stress on open competition, the nature of the market structure, and the character of the large corporation as an institution—are absent in other occupational settings. Some of these factors will be investigated in Chapter 3. Chapter 4 will look at the ways in which businessmen justify and rationalize their violations of the law. Although some of these justifications are present in other occupational groups, a number of them are closely tied to the enterprise of business. The last two chapters will assess the response of the criminal justice system to business crime and suggest reforms of that system. The legal system's response to business crime is more elaborate than its response to other types of occupational crime; indeed, some other occupations are defined as professions in part because they are self-regulating, although the effectiveness of self-regulation by lawyers and physicians may well be questioned.

Occupational crime by professionals differs in other important ways from crime in the business world. Professionals are screened by standards of admission prior to undertaking specialized training in a body of knowledge and theory (e.g., law or medicine), they are tested by an organized professional group before being licensed to practice, they learn a sense of duty, and they are regulated by a code of professional ethics which may lead to sanctions, including disqualification from practice. Because of their expertise, professionals are in a better position than their clients to know what their clients need; as a result, professionals are often entrusted with wide discretion. Financial return is supposedly not the primary objective for a professional; instead, service is paramount. Although these aspects of a profession are ideals, they do influence practitioners in important ways. Businessmen are different. Anyone with capital (including gangsters and others with prior criminal records) can begin or enter a legitimate business. No specialized academic training is needed, nor are businessmen screened or licensed to engage in their work. Existing codes of business ethics are vague, unenforced, and without practical effect. The customer's desires generally guide the businessman, although advertising is used to influence those desires; in contrast, professionals are often prevented from advertising their services by their codes of ethics. Also, financial return is the primary objective for the businessman, although he may hold other goals as well.

The types of behavior we shall be concerned with in this book are diverse: corporate antitrust actions, stock and security frauds and thefts, embezzlement and employee theft, consumer fraud and deceitful practices such as false and misleading advertising, bribery of government officials by businessmen, tax fraud in the business world, and black market violations of government regulations which establish ceiling prices and ration goods. Some of these crimes involve losses to the public, stockholders, and competitors; others involve losses to the corporation at the hands of employees; and others are illegal forms of behavior which do not involve any clear-cut victim. Al Capone once referred to these offenses collectively as "the legitimate rackets."[46]

[46]Cited in Vold, *Theoretical Criminology*, p. 245.

two

Business Crime and the Public

The issue of public norms and attitudes toward business crime has long formed a central part of the debate over whether white collar crime should be considered criminal in the same way as are such offenses as murder and rape. For Sutherland, public attitudes were not critical in defining crime, although he was aware that such attitudes might affect the types of sanctions used for violations of the law.[1] However, Sutherland implicitly introduced public attitudes toward business crimes into his definition of white collar crime by saying that white collar criminals were "respectable"; white collar offenders were by definition held in high regard by the public.

Public attitudes toward business crime have been important in the conceptualization of white collar crime since Sutherland's original study. "Crime" has been viewed as an offender's violation of the "existing tolerance limits of the community" rather than as an objective fact about behavior.[2] One sociologist opposed the treatment of OPA violators in the Detroit meat industry as criminals because they were not regarded by society as criminals.[3] Another scholar has argued that the laws defining white collar crime "have never been regarded generally by the

[1]Edwin H. Sutherland, *White Collar Crime* (New York: Holt, Rinehart and Winston, 1949, 1961), p. 9.

[2]Courtlandt Van Vechten, "The Tolerance Quotient as a Device for Defining Certain Social Concepts," *American Journal of Sociology*, 46 (July 1940), 38.

[3]Ernest W. Burgess, "Comment," *American Journal of Sociology*, 56 (July 1950), 34.

community as of the same kind, to be handled in the same way, as those involving the historic common law crimes."[4] These students of crime all assert that the public does not regard white collar crime as real crime; however, they produce no empirical support for their contentions.

There is widespread acceptance of the view that the public is "condoning, indifferent, or ambivalent" toward business crime.[5] This view goes back at least as far as 1907, when E. A. Ross said that the acts of "criminaloids" were not under the "effective ban of public opinion" and that their behavior was not stigmatized by the public, the press, or the government in the same way as traditional crime. He suggested that the "backwardness of public opinion" might nullify the effect of the law; with public morality lagging behind legislation, business offenders would have more opportunity to prey on the public.[6] More recently, occupational crime has been distinguished from other crimes in "the toleration and support it receives from the public."[7]

Although the common view that the public is tolerant of business crime may not necessarily be true, the feeling that it is true may have consequences for the legal treatment of white collar offenders. Prosecutors may not bring a case against an offender because they sense that juries do not want to put businessmen in jail. One district attorney who was asked by an Attorney General to prosecute a fraudulent operator replied, "I can't even get a conviction when they stick a gun in somebody's back, how can I get one when they just talk him out of his money."[8] Failure to seek a conviction because of a belief in public tolerance of business crime may reduce the deterrent effect of the law and increase the amount of such crime.

If the public is indeed tolerant of business crime, it may be because the offenses themselves and their impact on the society are difficult to comprehend. White collar crime "is usually more complex and diffused over a longer period of time than is the case with ordinary crimes, and

[4]George B. Vold, *Theoretical Criminology* (New York: Oxford University Press, 1958), p. 259.

[5]Vilhelm Aubert, "White Collar Crime and Social Structure," *American Journal of Sociology*, 58 (November 1952), 265.

[6]Edward Alsworth Ross, *Sin and Society: An Analysis of Latter-Day Iniquity* (Boston: Houghton Mifflin, 1907), pp. 69-70.

[7]Marshall B. Clinard and Richard Quinney, *Criminal Behavior Systems: A Typology* (New York: Holt, Rinehart and Winston, 1967), p. 137.

[8]Cited in "Translating Sympathy for Deceived Consumers into Effective Programs for Protection," *University of Pennsylvania Law Review*, 114 (January 1966), 426-27.

this fact obscures the essential criminality of the acts."[9] Stock fraud and manipulation are often complex undertakings beyond the understanding of the average investor. The computer mystique—the notion that "the computer made a mistake" is a sufficient explanation for erroneous billing or missing assets—is a result of the complexity of modern computers and the inability of people to understand how they actually function.

People may be relatively indifferent toward crime in the business world because they fail to understand its real costs. They may view business offenses as civil wrongs or torts rather than as crimes. They may feel there is little real harm involved in most business crime; in a wealthy society such as the United States the relatively small financial loss for any given victim in any given crime may seem a small price to pay for a productive economy. There is a problem in placing a dollar value on losses which result from such offenses as a slight misrepresentation in advertising or a price-fixing conspiracy. In times of rapid inflation, increased costs to consumers resulting from business crimes are concealed in the generally rising prices and are not apt to elicit public outrage. When the victim's loss is covered by insurance, condemnation will be minimal because the victim does not seem to have suffered any real harm. Since business crime is often covert, it frequently does not involve a confrontation between the victim and the offender and it rarely includes any violence. As a result, people are often unaware of the crime or only mildly condemning if they do know of it. People may also see business crime as an intrinsic part of commerce, whereas they view traditional crime as uncalled for. Also, the corporation, being intangible, may elicit less condemnation than the traditional offender, who is easier to picture and thus a better target for outrage.[10]

Public reaction to white collar crime may occasionally be intense if the violation is flagrant, a large sum of money is involved, and a large and well-known corporation is the offender. One such case did occur in 1961, a conspiracy by a number of large electrical companies to fix prices. However, no systematic survey of public opinion was conducted to tap public reaction to this case. Public reaction to less dramatic crimes in the business world is apt to be minimal, just as reactions to petty

[9]Clinard and Quinney, *Criminal Behavior Systems*, p. 137.
[10]Christopher D. Stone, *Where the Law Ends* (New York: Harper & Row, Publishers, 1975), p. 248.

larcenies or minor misdemeanors are usually minimal. That people will sometimes treat business offenses as seriously as they treat traditional crime was revealed in a statement by a juror in a civil case in which $1.2 million was awarded to a plaintiff who had sued a company: "Any criminal is certainly punished for his crimes, and this we felt was a crime so far as the company was concerned."[11]

Yet another reason to expect public ambivalence toward business crimes is that the victim of many such crimes is a competitor rather than a private citizen. Antitrust offenses may not seem especially reprehensible to the public because the victims appear to be other corporations, although anticompetitive practices actually raise prices for all consumers. Also, the public may not be especially outraged at the news of an embezzlement, since the victim seems to be the company which hired the worker in the first place, although losses may be passed on to customers in the form of higher prices. People have difficulty empathizing with the large corporation as a victim of a crime. When forced to make a choice of a victim from which they would steal, people prefer to steal from a large business concern rather than from the government, and from the government rather than from a small business concern.[12] Choice of victim is predicated on the widely held view that theft from a large business concern involves the least evil and the least risk; theft from the government is thought to involve somewhat more risk, and theft from a small business concern is thought to entail considerable risk and to be reprehensible as well. Theft from large corporations is viewed as least wicked because they are seen as impersonal bureaucracies which are inefficient and do not serve the public well. This view has probably become even more widespread in recent years with the development of the "rip-off mentality" than was true when research into the problem was done twenty years ago.

---

[11]Cited in Sanford J. Ungar, "Get Away with What You Can," in Robert L. Heilbroner and others, *In the Name of Profit: Profiles in Corporate Irresponsibility* (Garden City, N.Y.: Doubleday & Company, Inc., 1972), p. 124.

[12]Erwin O. Smigel, "Public Attitudes toward Stealing as Related to the Size of the Victim Organization," *American Sociological Review*, 21 (June 1956), 320–27. Also, a recent poll asking American citizens about the honesty and integrity of different institutions found that small businesses were second only to banks, but that large businesses ranked sixteenth on the list; the author attributes this difference to the better communication between customer and businessman in small business organizations. See Thomas A. Murphy, "Mr. Murphy Takes the Blame," *The New York Times*, October 10, 1976, Section 3, p. 16.

Studies of Public Opinion toward Business Crime

Some scholars have refused to make assumptions regarding what public attitudes toward business crime are. They suggest that those attitudes may change over time, and they call for studies of the real nature of public opinion toward business crime rather than easy assumptions about that opinion.[13] There are a limited number of empirical investigations of the actual state of public norms and attitudes toward crime in the business world.

One study which examined attitudes toward white collar offenders as a general category was based on questionnaires filled out by 305 freshmen and sophomores at a Southern university.[14] This survey found that knowledge of white collar crime was quite limited: only 42 percent of the sample had read or heard about white collar crime and only 32 percent could give an adequate definition of the term. The popular image of the white collar criminal was a "rather innocuous figure" who was "educated, neat, male, clean, white, and married"; however, he was also "dishonest, ambitious, intelligent, greedy, and aggressive."[15] Lack of media exposure to white collar crime may have been partially responsible for the less elaborate image and the less objectionable nature of the white collar offender, in contrast to perceptions of conventional criminals held by the same sample. When asked what they feared most about white collar crime, the students referred to being cheated, embarrassed, or physically harmed; however, only 40 percent gave such responses, the rest being uncertain about the consequences of business crime.

There was a smaller social distance between the student respondent and the white collar offender than between the respondent and the con-

[13]See William N. Hannay, "Introduction to a Symposium on White-Collar Crime," *The American Criminal Law Review*, 11 (Summer 1973), 819; Hermann Mannheim, *Comparative Criminology* (Boston: Houghton Mifflin Company, 1965), p. 480; Gilbert Geis, "Toward a Delineation of White Collar Offenses," *Sociological Inquiry*, 32 (Spring 1962), 248; and Louis Galambos, *The Public Image of Big Business in America, 1880-1940* (Baltimore: The Johns Hopkins University Press, 1975). Through a content analysis of eleven journals, Galambos demonstrates that public attitudes toward large corporations and their behavior changed markedly over the period from 1880 to 1940.

[14]John P. Reed and Robin S. Reed, "Doctor, Lawyer, Indian Chief: Old Rhymes and New on White Collar Crime," *International Journal of Criminology and Penology*, 3 (August 1975), 279-93.

[15]*Ibid.*, p. 282.

ventional criminal. When asked to recommend criminal penalties for
white collar offenders, students usually preferred suspended sentences,
probation, fines, or short prison terms. The two major exceptions—
embezzlement and causing a death because of failure to repair a dwelling
unit—were more commonly met with long prison sentences.[16] These
two offenses were regarded as seriously as bank robbery; 53 percent of
the students recommended a long prison term or the death penalty for a
bank robber, 55 percent recommended similar punishments for a bank
officer who embezzled a large amount of money, and 50 percent recommended similar punishments for a landlord whose failure to repair a
building caused a tenant's death. Such harsh penalties were recommended
by 40 percent of the students for a broker who knowingly sold fraudulent
securities, and by 15 percent for a corporate executive who conspired
to restrain trade. In contrast, such sanctions were recommended by 1
percent of the students for shoplifting, 3 percent for drunk and disorderly
behavior, 10 percent for drug use, and 4 percent for sodomy. For two
other conventional crimes, murder (93 percent) and rape (72 percent),
most students recommended a long prison sentence or the death
penalty.[17] Background characteristics of the respondents were important
determinants of recommended penalties:

> For white collar offences, the harshest penalties were imposed by males,
> blacks, young adults, non-flag flyers, students with fathers in clerical,
> sales and blue-collar occupations, non-social science majors, rurals and
> small city dwellers, non-church attenders and non-members. Their cate-
> gorical counterparts were more lenient.[18]

This study of student attitudes toward white collar offenders may be
criticized for drawing conclusions from a sample of the population
which has had little experience in the world of work. An unusual study
by Rettig and Pasamanick permits an exploration of changes in moral
attitudes toward certain business crimes as a function of adult socialization.[19] This study questioned respondents about the rightness or

[16]*Ibid.*, p. 286.

[17]*Ibid.*

[18]*Ibid.*, p. 287.

[19]Salomon Rettig and Benjamin Pasamanick, "Changes in Moral Values as a Function
of Adult Socialization," *Social Problems*, 7 (Fall 1959), 117–25; Salomon Rettig and Benjamin Pasamanick, "Changes in Moral Values over Three Decades, 1929-1958," *Social
Problems*, 6 (Spring 1959), 320–28.

wrongness of 50 different types of behavior. Of the five items which involve business crime, four were among the 25 items eliciting the most moral condemnation. Also, three of those five items (charging interest above a fair rate for loans, misrepresenting the value of an investment to a potential investor, and maintaining working conditions which are known to be detrimental to employees' health) showed a pattern of declining moral condemnation with increasing age; the fourth (a strong commercial concern selling below cost to crowd out a weaker competitor) showed a pattern of stable moral condemnation with increasing age; and the fifth (setting a vacant building on fire in order to collect insurance) showed a pattern of increasing moral condemnation with increasing age.[20] Although these data are limited, they suggest that moral condemnation of business crime may decline somewhat as a result of adult socialization.

Another survey which measured public attitudes toward business crime questioned an "informal quota sample of [320] community residents" in the San Francisco area.[21] In this study, Gibbons presented hypothetical situations to respondents to determine how they would like to see various offenders punished. In general, people desired harsher punishments than were commonly handed down by the courts. Seventy percent of the sample felt that a prison sentence should be given to an antitrust violator; 43 percent favored a prison term for an advertiser who misrepresented his product. In comparison, 70 percent favored a prison sentence for auto theft, and 48 percent favored such a penalty for an assault. These data suggest that public views toward at least these two business crimes are similar to attitudes toward two crimes which appear in the FBI's index of serious crimes.

Information on comparative judgments about white collar crime and conventional crime is also provided by a 1969 Louis Harris poll. In making comparative judgments, "[c]ommon criminals, militants and the sexually promiscuous almost always came out better across the entire Harris sample than the prototypical Establishment figure who violates a trust."[22] For example, people felt that a manufacturer of unsafe cars is worse than a robber (by 68 percent to 22 percent), that a white grocer

[20]*Ibid.*

[21]Don C. Gibbons, "Crime and Punishment: A Study of Social Attitudes," *Social Forces,* 47 (June 1969), 395.

[22]"Changing Morality: The Two Americas: A *Time*-Louis Harris Poll," *Time,* 93 (June 6, 1969), 26.

who sells bad meat to a black customer is worse than a black rioter (by 63 percent to 22 percent), and that a businessman who illegally fixes prices is worse than a burglar (by 54 percent to 28 percent). Harris concluded, "Analysis of this list leaves little doubt that immoral acts committed by Establishment figures are viewed as much worse, by and large, than anti-Establishment figures who have caused all the recent flurries of public indignation."[23] This survey was conducted during a time of great public concern with "crime in the streets" and predated the era of Watergate and other government and business scandals.

A 1976 Gallup poll provides more recent evidence about public attitudes toward the honesty of businessmen.[24] A cross section of American adults rated business executives and advertising executives quite low in honesty and ethical standards, in comparison to other occupational groups. The following shows the proportion of the sample of 1,524 adults who ranked each of various groups high or very high in ethical standards:

Medical doctors	55%
Engineers	48%
College teachers	44%
Journalists	33%
Lawyers	25%
Building contractors	22%
Business executives	19%
Senators	19%
Congressmen	14%
Labor union leaders	13%
Advertising executives	11%

These two surveys suggest that the American businessman is not the highly revered member of the community which many have assumed him to be.

A study by Newman asked 178 people to recommend penalties for offenders involved in violations of a long-established law against business crime—the Food, Drug and Cosmetic Act of 1906.[25] The violations included the misbranding of food, the sale of "aesthetically adulterated" (distasteful but not harmful) food, and the sale of adulterated food

[23]*Ibid.*

[24]"High Rating Given to Doctors in Poll," *The New York Times,* August 22, 1976, p. 32.

[25]Donald J. Newman, "Public Attitudes toward a Form of White-Collar Crime," *Social Problems,* 4 (January 1953), 228–32.

which was harmful. Respondents were told the facts of the case and were informed that there had been a conviction; they were then asked to recommend a penalty. Nearly four of every five subjects felt that the penalty meted out should have been more severe than it was; the rest thought that the penalty should have been the same or less. Although respondents favored stronger penalties than the ones actually given, only one of every five favored a penalty which was harsher than allowed by existing law. Thus the range of penalties allowed by law encompassed the penalties recommended by four-fifths of the sample, although most of the subjects felt that the actual penalty meted out was too lenient. These findings imply more public condemnation of business crime than some sociologists have assumed to exist, but they also indicate that the public generally supports existing laws, if not the way in which those laws are actually enforced.

Although Sutherland suggested that there is more tolerance for white collar crime among people of higher socioeconomic status, Newman found no significant variations by income or education. This may be because the norm which was violated was that industry should produce goods which are safe for consumer use. Such a norm, and the related value of human health and safety, may be more widely shared and understood at all levels of social class than the norms which are violated in such offenses as restraint of trade and unfair labor practices. Respondents probably called for harsher penalties than were usually meted out because their expectations of proper business exchanges were violated in the cases presented to them. In other words, they expected that a customer would exchange money for a product which was properly labeled and unadulterated. Reaction to a breach of this normative expectation may vary with the type of business exchange, so that response to the sale of contaminated food may be stronger than response to sale of a defective used car. People expect to buy food which will not make them sick, but they may expect that some used car dealers will be less than completely honest. The fact that people distinguish between types of businessmen in terms of honesty is suggested by a Gallup poll which found that a new car dealer was ranked last in honesty and trustworthiness among seven types of businessmen.[26]

[26]Cited in William N. Leonard and Marvin Glenn Weber, "Automakers and Dealers: A Study of Criminogenic Market Forces," *Law and Society Review,* 4 (February 1970), 413-14.

There was much speculation about public attitudes toward violations of OPA regulations during and after World War II. Some observers assumed that the public favored the controls but others argued that it was public demand which created the extensive black market. Surveys between 1941 and 1945 showed strong public support for the regulations, with support ranging from a minimum of two-thirds to a maximum of 97 percent of a national sample.[27] One survey found variations in support by occupation: 80 percent of the laborers favored the controls, compared to 68 percent of the white collar workers, 61 percent of the farmers, and 53 percent of the businessmen. Those most negatively affected by the regulations opposed them the most, although a majority of all occupational groups favored the controls.[28] Wealthier individuals were less supportive of the regulations, although they also had more money with which to purchase costly black market goods.

One government official speaking in 1943 incorrectly assumed that public support for the OPA regulations was lacking, and he was even able to provide the following explanation for that supposed lack of support:

> The public is, to a large extent, doubtful of the need for OPA regulations, ignorant of their provisions, and skeptical of their fairness. This is due to a number of factors. In large measure it can be attributed to unwarranted and unfair attacks by business interests, by congressmen and congressional committees, by newspapers, and by various pressure groups. Much of this stems from purely political motives.[29]

What this official may have had in mind was not public support for the regulations themselves, but rather public attitudes toward businessmen or consumers who violated the regulations. Although most people favored the price and rationing controls, they may also have been willing to overlook certain offenses and to categorize business offenders as different from "other criminals." There may also have been some reluctance to condemn businessmen during the wartime emergency when their services were needed. Violations were not always obviously contrary to public welfare, although they were inflationary and may have pro-

[27]Marshall B. Clinard, *The Black Market: A Study of White Collar Crime* (Montclair, N.J.: Patterson Smith, 1952, 1969), pp. 89–114.

[28]*Ibid.*, p. 92.

[29]*Ibid.*, pp. 328–29.

longed the war. Because the businessmen who violated the regulations rarely used force or threats to extort money, they were probably not seen as predatory or malicious. So, although there was general support for the OPA regulations, there was no harsh condemnation of the OPA violators themselves, except for those who violated ration currency regulations.[30]

Those who suggested that the public did not support the OPA regulations cited as evidence the public's regular violation of those regulations. Without citizens who were willing to buy black market goods, there would have been much less illegal traffic, although businessmen would have continued to pay illegally high prices to secure scarce goods. The public was often tolerant of small price increases above regulated levels, and they would often purchase goods without asking questions. Those who assumed that willingness to buy goods at illegal prices was indicative of opposition to the OPA regulations assumed a degree of consistency in public attitudes and public behavior which apparently did not exist.

Although the public verbally supported the regulations, it did not necessarily follow that they would favor government action against black marketeers. Indeed, people might even have supported the regulations *because* they were easily violated. About one-fifth of the public tolerated small amounts of black market activity, although most of them felt that such behavior was permissible only under emergency conditions such as illness or in instances of unfairness such as an uncooperative rationing board.[31] Violations were also justified on the grounds that the regulations went against such basic American values as free enterprise, the right to make a profit, and consumer freedom to strike a fair bargain. Most Americans supported the regulations and few engaged in systematic and long-term violations, although it is not clear if this was because of moral scruples or lack of opportunity.

Hartung's study of OPA violations in the Detroit meat industry casts additional light on public attitudes toward business crime. Forty meat company managers and 322 private citizens were asked to express, on a five-point scale, their approval or disapproval of ten different violations —five criminal cases and five civil cases. The private citizens reacted with similar degrees of disapproval to the civil and the criminal violations;

[30]*Ibid.*, p. 328.
[31]*Ibid.*, p. 93.

this result suggests that the public does not support legal differences in the handling of the cases. The managers were much more disapproving of the criminal violations than they were of the civil violations. The managers and the citizens disapproved of the five criminal violations to the same extent, but they differed significantly in their assessment of the five civil violations, with the public being much more disapproving than the managers. Hartung concluded that there were shared values on the behavior which was officially dealt with as crime, but disagreement on the behavior dealt with as civil violation.[32] This study suggests again a greater degree of public condemnation of business violations than is thought to exist by those who claim that the public is apathetic to or tolerant of business crime.

Studies of Public Opinion toward Employee Theft

One specific type of business crime which has been the basis for several studies of public opinion is employee theft, including embezzlement. Public reaction to this type of theft may be weaker than reaction to other kinds of larceny because of a belief that an employer is responsible for selecting and controlling his workers and that it is his own fault if he is victimized by one of those workers. Reaction may also be diminished because of the popular belief that employees will have to repay the company what they stole or that the company can easily absorb the loss if they fail to do so. Employee thefts may also be seen as "violations of specialized occupational norms" rather than as attacks upon basic societal values[33]; this attitude may result from the complex and apparently nonthreatening nature of the crimes. Public reaction may also be reduced by the lack of sympathy for the large, impersonal corporate victim. On the other hand, public reaction to employee theft might be greater than reaction to common larcenies because such a crime involves *both* an attack upon the sanctity of private property *and* a violation of trust by the employee.

[32]Frank E. Hartung, "Common and Discrete Values," *Journal of Social Psychology,* 38 (August 1953), 3–22.

[33]Daniel Glaser, "National Goals and Indicators for the Reduction of Crime and Delinquency," *The Annals of the American Academy of Political and Social Science,* 371 (May 1967), 114.

One pertinent study was carried out by Alfred Winslow Jones in Akron, Ohio, in the 1940s. This study included the following question:

> Anthracite coal mining in Eastern Pennsylvania was a "sick industry" even before the depression. In the 1930's still more mines shut down, the companies deciding to keep their coal in the ground until prices for it should go up. There was great unemployment and distress among the miners. In these years the unemployed miners began going into the idle mines and taking out the coal. They did this without the permission of the companies which own the mines, and without the interference of the local police, so that no violence resulted. They have both burned the coal themselves, and sold it.

> **Question.**
> What do you think of this sort of action on the part of the unemployed miners?
> **Answers.**
> 0. I approve.
> 1. I think it may have been all right if they were really in distress, but I'm doubtful about it.
> 2. I can't decide.
> 3. I suppose it is wrong, but I must qualify my feeling. For example, I think it wrong for them to sell the coal, but not if they merely burn it to keep warm.
> 4. I disapprove, and cannot let my sympathies interfere.[34]

Subjects were in effect asked to balance a number of conflicting social norms, including: (a) an individual may take any action to ensure the survival of himself and his family; (b) large corporations must take the public welfare into account in the exercise of their power; (c) theft is not justifiable if it is performed in an organized fashion for profit; and (d) any theft is wrong because it violates the law and threatens the system of private ownership of property. A number of respondents acknowledged the dilemma of weighing these competing norms.

A random sample of 303 Akron residents had a mean response score of 1.5. Only one in five selected the last choice of outright disapproval. A similar proportion chose response number 3, but most picked number 0, unqualified approval. The mean score of three groups of manual

[34]Alfred Winslow Jones, *Life, Liberty and Property* (New York: Octagon Books, Inc., 1941, 1964), p. 358.

workers (who were not part of the random sample of Akron residents) wàs 0.9; they were thus more approving of the miners' behavior than the sample of Akron residents. Both the manual workers and the random sample resolved the conflict among competing norms in favor of theft because of the strength of the norm of personal and family survival and because they felt that corporations should behave in a socially responsible manner. Various groups of middle-level and white collar workers had mean scores ranging from 1.0 to 2.0, expressing more disapproval of the theft than the manual workers but still favoring the theft of the coal. A group of eighteen businessmen and managers had a mean score of 3.7; fourteen of them chose alternative 4, unqualified disapproval. These businessmen felt that any theft of property was wrong and constituted a threat to the system of private ownership of property upon which the American economy was based. This study shows that the situation in which a theft occurs, as well as the motives for the theft, are important determinants of public reaction to crime, and also that a respondent's tolerance or condemnation of an offense will vary with his position in the social stratification system.

Additional evidence of public sentiments toward employee theft comes from a study of random samples of Danish men, women, and male prisoners.[35] Kutschinsky asked respondents to rank five different property crimes in terms of the length of sentence they would recommend for each offense. The following rankings by each group place the offense receiving the harshest recommended penalty at the top:

Men (N = 79)	Women (N = 58)	Male prisoners (N = 95)
1. Burglary	1. Check forgery vs. bank	1. Burglary
2. Theft at place of employment	2. Burglary	2. Theft at place of employment
3. Check forgery vs. bank	3. Theft at place of employment	3. Check forgery vs. bank
4. Fraud vs. a businessman	4. Fraud vs. a businessman	4. Fraud vs. a businessman
5. Tax evasion	5. Tax evasion	5. Tax evasion

[35]Berl Kutschinsky, "Knowledge and Attitudes Regarding Legal Phenomena in Denmark," in *Scandinavian Studies in Criminology: Aspects of Social Control in Welfare States,* ed. Nils Christie (London: Tavistock Publications, 1968), pp. 125-60.

Clearly there is substantial agreement in the rank orderings here; in fact, if check forgery had been ranked third instead of first by women, all three groups would have been in perfect agreement. It is difficult to account fully for these orderings. The size and impersonality of the government as victim may partially account for the ranking of tax evasion last by all groups. Employee theft may have been ranked relatively high because respondents condemned an offender who violated trust which had been placed in him by an employer. Only burglary, which involves invasion of privacy in addition to theft and which poses a risk to the occupant of a dwelling, was ranked higher than employee theft by the men and by the male prisoners. This relatively high degree of condemnation of employee theft suggests that corporate executives who must decide whether or not to prosecute employee thieves might enjoy more public support for prosecution than they think they would, although this study was done in Denmark and findings might be different in the United States.

Another study by Kutschinsky in Denmark involved the playing of two tape recordings which described crimes—one an employee theft and the other an assault—to nonrandom samples of 242 men and 107 women. He found only slight variations by social class in preferred punishments for the employee thief, with middle- and upper-class subjects being somewhat more severe than working-class subjects. Large proportions of all social classes chose to imprison or detain the thief; however, as the author notes, "That does not mean, of course, that a similar offence would not be tacitly accepted by workers in *daily life*, for it is highly conceivable that a change in attitude occurs toward 'accepted irregularities' the moment such a misdemeanour is discovered and reported."[36] In this regard, public reactions may be similar to those of the American public to OPA violations: verbal condemnation but tolerance when faced with actual violators of the law.

A 1968 survey of American attitudes toward various types of offenders also found a relatively high condemnation of one type of employee thief, the embezzler.[37] Representative samples of 1,000 adults and 200 teenagers were interviewed. They were asked what penalties they would recommend for each of a number of offenders. Their responses follow:

---

[36]*Ibid.*, p. 135.

[37]Joint Commission on Correctional Manpower and Training, *The Public Looks at Crime and Corrections* (Washington, D.C.: Joint Commission on Correctional Manpower and Training, 1968).

	Probation	Short jail sentence with parole	Long prison sentence	Not sure
Embezzler	7%	43%	42%	8%
Burglar	20%	57%	15%	8%
Armed robber	0%	11%	86%	3%
Prostitute	26%	36%	23%	15%
Murderer	0%	2%	90%	8%
Looter in riot	21%	46%	28%	5%
Seller of narcotics to a minor	0%	4%	94%	2%

On the basis of these recommended sentences, an embezzler is considered by the American public to be a less serious offender than an armed robber, a murderer, or a seller of narcotics to minors, but a more serious offender than a burglar, a prostitute, or a rioter who engages in looting. There were no differences in recommended sentences by respondents' age or sex. However, white respondents and more educated respondents preferred shorter sentences than their counterparts. However, even among white and more educated respondents, the level of condemnation of embezzlers was quite high in comparison with other offenders.

Respondents in this survey were also asked if they would feel uneasy if they knew they were working with a parolee who had been convicted of one of a series of crimes. The proportions who said they would are as follows:

Shooting someone in armed robbery	74%
Embezzling from a charity	41%
Passing bad checks	32%
Stealing an automobile	29%
Evading income tax payments	19%
Shoplifting at age 16	16%

The only offender who would evoke more uneasiness than the embezzler was someone who not only stole but also presented a direct threat of violence to his victim, an armed robber who shot someone during the commission of his crime.

Public attitudes toward employee theft were also tapped in Gibbons' study of San Francisco residents.[38] Respondents were asked to recommend punishments for an employee who "borrowed" over $15,000 from the company for which he worked, a case of embezzlement. A very large proportion of the subjects (88 percent) favored a prison sentence for the offender. In the 1968 national survey mentioned above, 85 percent favored a prison term for an accountant who was caught embezzling.[39] A survey of two Boston-area communities found that 46 percent of the interviewed residents of a low crime rate suburb and 54 percent of a sample from an urban community with a higher crime rate favored a prison sentence for "a bank manager [who] steals $100 from the vault in the bank in which he works."[40] Possibly the proportions are lower in this study because of the relatively trivial sum involved.

In general, surveys indicate a fairly high degree of public condemnation of employee theft and embezzlement, rather than the public ambivalence and tolerance suggested by many observers. Instead of being lenient toward high-status offenders who steal from large and impersonal organizations, many people favor the incarceration of such offenders to a greater degree than they do for those who commit traditional crimes. Public condemnation of employee theft was found in studies which questioned a variety of types of respondents. Such condemnation may be relatively strong and widespread because people react to the violation of trust as well as to the theft of property.

In summary, public opinion toward crime in the business world is a function of many factors, including attitudes toward trust violation, attitudes toward private property, empathy with the victim of the crime, expectations about business transactions with different types of businessmen, and feelings about extenuating circumstances. Characteristics of respondents such as age, sex, race, and social class may also influence views of certain business crimes. However, the sparse evidence which is currently available indicates a much stronger condemnation of business crime than has been commonly thought to exist.

More detailed studies are needed to assess accurately the nature of public attitudes toward business crime; in any event, it may be stated with some assurance that the public itself is not well-organized to fight

[38]Gibbons, "Crime and Punishment," p. 394.

[39]Joint Commission, *The Public Looks,* p. 11.

[40]John E. Conklin, *Public Reactions to Crime: A Survey of Two Communities* (Cambridge, Mass.: Harvard University, Ph.D. dissertation, 1969).

business crime. When asked about business crime in a survey, people may condemn such violations. However, they are rarely indignant or militant in the expression of their condemnation of business crime. They take their own exploitation for granted and feel they are helpless to rectify matters. Public attitudes have failed to coalesce in part because of the complex and diffuse nature of business crime, the absence of obvious victims, the small monetary losses for each victim, and the lack of continuing media attention to business crime. Because of the absence of a strong countervailing force, business offenders are subject to neither informal control by public opinion nor formal legal controls which would result from citizen action to have new laws passed and old ones enforced. Such circumstances set the stage for the perpetration of crime in the business world.

three

Business Crime
and the Economy

The American economic system is conducive to business crime in a number of ways. Some of these are the emphasis on consumption, the drive for profits, the nature of market conditions, the pervasiveness of trust relationships in the world of commerce, and the structure of the large corporation.

The Consumption-Oriented Economy

The genius of the American economy is less in the area of production than in the area of distribution; "America is a nation of salesmen."[1] Businessmen not only produce goods and services efficiently; they also create new demands effectively and exploit existing markets with skill. Some assert that they also trick consumers into wanting goods and services they would not want if they were not exposed to advertising and the hard sell. When the businessman confronts closed or saturated domestic markets, he finds other markets for his goods; for example, when cyclamates were banned in the United States, businessmen distributed foods containing cyclamates abroad where no restrictive rules existed.

Intense competition in an industry may lead businessmen to engage

[1]S. John Insulata, "Deceptive Business Practices: Criminals in Cuff Links," *Vital Speeches of the Day*, 29 (May 15, 1963), 473; also see Jean-Jacques Servan-Schreiber, *The American Challenge*, trans. Ronald Steel (New York: Atheneum, 1968).

in bribery or false advertising to sell their products. Bribes, kickbacks, and threats may be used to give a businessman's product a competitive advantage in the marketplace. For example, in the highly competitive and highly profitable record industry, there have been revelations about payments to disc jockeys and radio station executives in order to get records played. Meat companies sometimes pay bribes to supermarket managers and purchasers to induce them to stock their products. Some airline corporations have paid kickbacks to travel agencies which sell their tickets.

The desire for a competitive advantage may also lead to false or deceptive advertising. In his study of corporate crime, Sutherland found that 60 percent of the corporations he studied which advertised at all had engaged in misrepresentative advertising; some had sold dangerous products and others had made exaggerated claims for their products.[2] Other forms of deceptive advertising include making false distinctions between one's own product and similar products (e.g., claiming that one pain-killer is more effective than others[3]), implying results from the use of a product which are not forthcoming, making unsubstantiated claims for a product, and deceptive labeling or pricing.

Exactly what constitutes a crime in the area of advertising is unclear, although a willful attempt to deceive does constitute fraud. However, "puffing" or making excessive claims for a product may fall short of fraud. Automobile manufacturers and dealers who in their advertisements give prominent attention to Environmental Protection Agency data on gasoline mileage imply that the car will, or at least can, get such mileage. In fact, such mileage is rarely if ever achieved, in part because EPA tests are conducted in a laboratory rather than on the road. Such advertising is not necessarily false, since it usually indicates that the mileage ratings are estimates based on EPA tests and are not guaranteed. However, such advertising does seem to be deceptive.

Another form of advertising which falls short of criminal fraud involves the sale of land. Salesmen often use a hard sell that allows prospective buyers to make incorrect inferences about the land they are buying.[4]

---

[2]Edwin H. Sutherland, *White Collar Crime* (New York: Holt, Rinehart and Winston, 1949, 1961), p. 122.

[3]John D. Morris, "F.T.C. Assails Pain-Killer Ads; Says They Mislead the Public," *The New York Times,* April 20, 1972, pp. 1, 26.

[4]Benjamin T. Shuman and Edward S. Jaffry, "Government and the Installment Land Sales Contract," *State Government,* 36 (Summer 1963), 148-51.

This hard sell is also used by door-to-door salesmen to stimulate consumption. The sale of home repairs and improvements in this way often involves fraud and deception. Consumers lack the information to assess whether repairs are actually needed, and the scare tactics of some salesmen lead them to sign contracts for unneeded services. Such salesmen employ phony bargains, financial tricks, unhonored guarantees, exaggerated claims, misrepresented materials, and false information to sell their products. Their sales techniques, including "contests," referral sales, bait-and-switch tactics, model houses, and discount prices, range from the unscrupulous to the criminal. Similar tactics are used by merchants such as furniture salesmen to induce customers to make unintended purchases. The bait-and-switch tactic, in which a customer is induced into a store by a low-priced item only to be told that the product is no longer in stock and that he would do well to buy a better-quality product which costs only a bit more, is one technique used by such merchants. Deceptive tagging of products may create the sense that the customer is faced with a bargain which is too good to pass up. Pricing and labeling may also be a problem, especially in grocery stores. One study found considerable confusion among a group of college-educated women in picking the most economical package of a given product.[5] Many of them paid higher per-unit prices for the product than was necessary. This seemed to result from poorly presented information on the packages, from misleading information as to quantity and quality of the contents, from misleading pricing information, and from the use of fractional numbers to indicate quantity.

One case of fraudulent advertising to stimulate consumption is the case of the Dale car, an automobile which was to get 70 miles per gallon and cost less than $2,000. The promotion of this three-wheeled car was successful because it came at a time of rising gasoline prices, rapid inflation, and high unemployment rates; the promised product met a consumption demand for a low-cost and efficient car. Options to buy the car and car distributorships were sold by the president of the corporation. He was arrested in 1975 and charged with conspiracy to commit theft; soon after, the corporation was placed in receivership.[6]

---

[5]Monroe P. Friedman, "Consumer Confusion in the Selection of Supermarket Products," *Journal of Applied Psychology,* 50 (December 1966), 529-34.

[6]Elliott Carlson, with Sunde Smith and Dudley Lynch, "Tale of the Dale," *Newsweek,* 85 (March 3, 1975), 60-61.

Because of the vague nature of the law regarding advertising, businessmen may be uncertain as to what they may do to sell their products. Some acts are clearly illegal, whereas others are unethical and still others of questionable morality. In one study, a group of twenty undergraduate students of corporate finance in a business administration program were asked about legal but clearly immoral advertising of interest rates.[7] Only three felt that the obvious and deliberate attempt to deceive the customer was immoral; eight felt that such advertising might or might not be immoral; eight felt that such advertising was not immoral; and the other one avoided the issue of morality in his response. Many of the students seemed to feel that it was acceptable to deceive an ignorant public even if the action were immoral.

The consumption mentality that results in part from advertising is conducive to business crime, as well as productive of traditional property offenses.[8] Most investigators who have studied the crime of embezzlement have concluded that it often results from an attempt to achieve or maintain a lifestyle which is beyond the means of the thief. A study of the experience of twenty surety companies with firms they had insured found that the two major causes of embezzlement were gambling (especially when a large sum was embezzled) and extravagant living standards (living beyond one's means or careless spending). Of lesser importance were unusual family expenses (such as medical emergencies), undesirable associates, and an inadequate income in bad economic times.[9] Questioning of incarcerated middle-class thieves in England—three-fourths of whom were in prison for such white collar offenses as embezzlement, forgery, tax evasion, and bankruptcy—found that 41 percent of them overspent their income in competing for social status, 21 percent had encountered business failures, 21 percent had low or irregular incomes, 16 percent had heavy financial liabilities at home, 15 percent had gambling debts, and 9 percent had drinking problems.[10] Again, spend-

[7]Bertrand N. Bauer, "Truth in Lending: College Business Students' Opinions of *Caveat Emptor*, Fraud and Deception," *American Business Law Journal*, 4 (Fall 1966), 156–61.

[8]For a discussion of the role of the media in the genesis of deviant behavior of various types, see Robert K. Merton, *Social Theory and Social Structure*, rev. and enlarged ed. (New York: The Free Press, 1957), pp. 166–70.

[9]Virgil W. Peterson, "Why Honest People Steal," *Journal of Criminal Law and Criminology*, 38 (July-August 1947), 94–103.

[10]G. E. Levens, "101 British White Collar Criminals," *New Society*, March 26, 1964, pp. 6–8.

ing beyond one's level of income emerges as an important cause of embezzlement; such spending is encouraged in a consumption-oriented economy which relies on advertising to stimulate consumer demand.

A study of embezzlers in the United States just after World War II found that male thieves stole for the following reasons, in order of importance: gambling or drinking, living above their means, having a criminal character, being poor business managers, and earning inadequate income. The typical male embezzler was 35 years old, was married, had one or two children, lived in a respectable neighborhood, and was in the process of buying his home. He was in the top 40 percent of American families in income, had worked for his employer for about three years, and had been stealing for about eight months when he was caught. The proceeds of his theft increased his annual income by 20 percent. Female embezzlers, who constituted 15 percent of the sample of thieves, stole because they were living above their means, had incurred family expenses, were extravagent (especially on clothes), had a criminal background, were influenced by male accomplices, or had experienced an illness in their family. The average female embezzler had an income in the bottom third of the national distribution and equaled her annual salary in the money she stole, although she stole less than the average male embezzler. She was 31 years old, was or had been married, had worked for her employer for two and a half years, and had been stealing for six and a half months when she was apprehended.[11] A more recent portrait of securities thieves is similar to the above picture of the embezzler. The typical securities thief is a trusted employee who is a white male, in his thirties and who has been on the job for two years and earns about $150 a week by working long hours. He is commonly in debt, often due to sports betting, which makes him vulnerable to the influence of organized crime figures who wish to fence stolen securities.[12]

A clear example of an embezzler who was living well beyond his means and was also involved in gambling is a chief teller in a bank who was arrested in 1973 for the theft of $1.5 million. He was earning $11,000 a year but was spending as much as $30,000 a day on gambling. The discovery of his theft came from an investigation of his bookie rather

[11]"Postwar Embezzler Is Younger, Lives Faster, Is Less Inclined to Suicide," *Journal of Accountancy,* 90 (October 1950), 344.

[12]Robert J. Cole, "How Crime Is Infiltrating Wall Street," *The New York Times,* November 30, 1969, Section 3, pp. 1, 11.

than from the disclosure of any wrongdoing at the bank. The teller was able to conceal his theft by juggling accounts in the bank's computer and by feeding the computer inaccurate information.[13]

When financial obligations beyond one's means are incurred and when the opportunity to embezzle funds to meet those obligations is available, people in positions of trust may steal those funds. Often the salaries of embezzlers are well below what their friends and families believe they are earning; they therefore conceal the fact that they cannot afford the lifestyle which they are trying to maintain. This may be a particular problem for individuals who are promoted into responsible executive positions without receiving commensurate salary increases. Structurally, the problem of embezzlement is related to the heavy emphasis on consumption in American society and to the emphasis on solving problems as individuals. Higher rates of embezzlement might be predicted in the American economy than in economies which are less oriented toward creating a demand for consumer goods (e.g., the People's Republic of China) or more oriented toward the family or work groups (e.g., Japan).

In his study of incarcerated embezzlers, Donald R. Cressey found that they had not only faced a financial problem (which was not necessarily due to extravagant living), but that the problem was seen by them as nonshareable, i.e., they could not share the problem with others who might have lent financial assistance. The problem might be non-shareable because the embezzler felt that his financial position was due to personal failure. It might also be nonshareable because it was due to business reversals which were the result of external causes but which he felt reflected poorly on his business acumen; "[v] alues in regard to success and profit-making are such that some individuals cannot even *think* of revealing a shaky business condition to anyone."[14] The problem might also be nonshareable because the embezzler felt that the cause of his financial difficulty was inconsistent with his role as a trusted employee; debts due to gambling or a mistress cannot be revealed by a trusted employee who is concerned with maintaining his status within the community.

---

[13]Lacey Fosburgh, "Chief Teller Is Accused of Theft of $1.5-Million at a Bank Here," *The New York Times,* March 23, 1973, pp. 1, 42; Donn B. Parker, *Crime by Computer* (New York: Charles Scribner's Sons, 1976), pp. 192-203.

[14]Donald R. Cressey, *Other People's Money: A Study in the Social Psychology of Embezzlement* (Belmont, Calif.: Wadsworth Publishing Co., 1953, 1971), p. 50.

A study of 100 Swedish embezzlers supports Cressey's conclusions. This study revealed that embezzlers often face late-life crises which lead to embezzlement. Declines in their careers are viewed as necessitating additional funds to solve problems of bankruptcy, personal debts, and family emergencies. Career instability, such as the inability to hold a job or frequent changes in jobs, leads to insecurity and financial difficulty. Overwork and exhaustion sometimes cause workers to become indifferent to the consequences of their crimes. Family problems such as marital conflict or the death of a relative were also cited as reasons for theft, as were the desire to protect social status and to preserve a business enterprise.[15]

Gwynn Nettler disagrees with Cressey's conclusion that the cause of embezzlement is always a nonshareable financial problem, claiming that this is an after-the-fact interpretation rather than a precondition of the violation of trust.[16] He says that almost any "frailty of life" can be fitted into Cressey's vague category of nonshareable problem. Five of the six cases of large-scale embezzlement which Nettler examined were inconsistent with Cressey's theory. In those cases, embezzlement arose from a combination of intense desire for money and opportunity to fulfill that desire, rather than from a nonshareable financial problem and the opportunity to solve it. The embezzlers sought extra but unneeded funds; as Aristotle once wrote, "the greatest crimes are not committed in order to acquire the necessary, but the superfluous."[17] Nettler found that embezzlement did produce a nonshareable financial embarrassment after the crime, but that problem resulted more from succumbing to the temptation to live beyond one's means than from having a financial problem which could not be shared with others.

The emphasis on consumption which leads to living beyond one's means also affects the poor in an especially acute manner. The poor receive the same message to consume which the middle class receives, and they may have the added inducement of a need to compensate for blocked social mobility.[18] A major source of the message to consume is

---

[15]Svend H. Riemer, "Embezzlement: Pathological Basis," *Journal of Criminal Law and Criminology*, 32 (November-December 1941), 411–23.

[16]Gwynn Nettler, "Embezzlement without Problems," *British Journal of Criminology*, 14 (January 1974), 70–77.

[17]Cited in Herbert A. Bloch and Gilbert Geis, *Man, Crime and Society*, 2nd ed. (New York: Random House, 1970), p. 307.

[18]David Caplovitz, *The Poor Pay More: Consumer Practices of Low-Income Families* (New York: The Free Press, 1967), p. 13.

television; almost all American homes now have sets. The poor are by definition less able than the middle class to consume in the manner urged on them by advertising. Not only do they lack the money with which to buy goods, but they also lack information on buying alternatives and they have not had the experience to be effective and sophisticated consumers. Because of the central role of credit in the American economy—a factor conducive to business crime which will be examined later in this chapter—the poor are provided with the means to purchase goods, even though they are often poor credit risks because of their low and unstable incomes. This situation is conducive to such consumer offenses as default on debt payments and to such business crimes against them as illegal interest rates.

Competition and Profit

The dominant ideology of American business is free enterprise. This ideology incorporates two sometimes incompatible elements: the pursuit of profits, and open competition among sellers. The stimulation of consumption through advertising and salesmanship serves the goal of corporate profitability. Profitability is regarded as the primary if not the exclusive goal of the business enterprise, rather than as a means to some other goal. This was stated bluntly by a bank vice-president in 1958:

> The goal of a business corporation is to make a profit. . . . *the only goal* of a business corporation is to make a profit. . . . *more fully,* the only goal of a business corporation is to make *the maximum possible profit.* . . . *Completely,* the only goal of a business corporation is to make the maximum possible profit *over a long period.*[19]

Some defenders of business argue that profit maximization is not the only goal, perhaps not even the primary goal of the corporation. Instead, they assert that the corporation seeks a "satisfactory profit."[20] The goal of the corporation is "to use its resources as efficiently as possible in supplying goods and services to its customers and to compensate equitably

[19]Cited in Fred J. Cook, *The Corrupted Land: The Social Morality of Modern America* (New York: Macmillan Publishing Co., Inc., 1966), p. 93. Emphasis in original.

[20]For example, see Robert M. Anthony, "The Trouble with Profit Maximization," *Harvard Business Review,* 38 (November-December 1960), 126–34.

those who supply these resources."[21] Arguments such as this point to such nonprofitable corporate activities as charitable donations, fringe benefits for employees, and severance pay to show that businessmen are socially responsible citizens rather than ruthless profitmongers. A survey of 1,700 *Harvard Business Review* readers who were business executives found that 94 percent felt that businessmen were not only out to make a profit. However, in response to a question about business ethics, they stated that ethics were a matter of "good business"; this response suggests that ethical behavior was regarded more as good public relations conducive to sales and profits rather than as an end in itself.[22] Nonprofitable ventures by businessmen can be interpreted without too much cynicism as efforts to create "goodwill" with the public and thus to enhance profitability and attract the best employees.

The goals of the corporation may also be seen as a hierarchy. The primary goal is survival of the enterprise. Next comes maintenance of a satisfactory profit level. Only then can the directors concern themselves with employee satisfaction, expansion of the enterprise, prestige of the firm, innovations in products, maintenance of an exciting internal work environment, and a socially responsible orientation.[23] Although companies are not exclusively oriented toward profits, probably the vast majority of business enterprises are either fighting for survival or trying to maintain a satisfactory profit level; hence, most corporations will concentrate the bulk of their efforts on maximizing profitability.

Evidence of a corporation's being concerned with factors other than profitability appears in an internal memorandum issued by General Electric a number of years ago. The following list gives eight "Key Result Areas" to be examined in measuring the performance of managers:

1. Profitability.
2. Market position.
3. Productivity, or the effective utilization of humans, capital, and material resources.
4. Product leadership.

[21]*Ibid.*, p. 128.

[22]Raymond C. Baumhart, "How Ethical Are Businessmen?" *Harvard Business Review*, 39 (July-August 1961), 5-17, 156-76.

[23]Christopher D. Stone, *Where the Law Ends* (New York: Harper & Row, Publishers, 1975), pp. 38-39.

5. Personnel development.
6. Employee attitudes.
7. Public responsibility.
8. Balance between short-range and long-range goals.[24]

Although the memorandum does not state it, this list appears to be in descending order of importance; it is difficult to imagine the firm rewarding workers who act in a publicly responsible but unprofitable manner.

There is disagreement over the extent to which corporations should be responsible for the social consequences of their actions. The chairman of Standard Oil of New Jersey once said, "A clear sense of responsibility to and integration with the public welfare is a prerequisite to successful business management in today's complex world."[25] On the other hand, Henry Ford II has said:

> I do not agree that the time has come, or is likely ever to come, when a corporation should assume social or political or other non-business roles. I believe business corporations will continue to serve society best as individual companies vie to achieve long-range profitability consistent with the public interest.[26]

If private corporations had the responsibility for the public welfare, there would be the problem of their having the power to decide what is best for the public without, however, being accountable to the public as politicians are. On the other hand, it is reasonable to expect a corporation to abstain from producing goods which are clearly harmful to consumers.

The exact link between the drive for profits and business crime is difficult to specify. Obviously not all corporations and businessmen engage in crime, even though they seek a profit. There is some evidence that when businessmen face a situation of declining or unstable profits, they may turn to crime to shore up their position. A writer at the turn of the century stated that businessmen turn to crime to retrieve their finan-

[24]Clarence C. Walton and Frederick W. Cleveland, Jr., *Corporations on Trial: The Electric Cases* (Belmont, Calif.: Wadsworth Publishing Co., 1964), p. 72.

[25]Cited in Walter Goodman, *All Honorable Men: Corruption and Compromise in American Life* (Boston: Little, Brown, 1963), p. 84.

[26]Cited in Goodman, *All Honorable Men*, p. 79.

cial losses and to save their companies when business gets bad.[27] A study of New England shoe manufacturers found that fair trade practice laws were violated most frequently when profits were declining.[28] There is also evidence that during recessions when profits drop, some businessmen "sell out to the insurance company" by setting fire to their plants and collecting on their insurance policies. Currently arson annually accounts for upwards of $1 billion in losses, defrauding insurance companies and costing thousands of workers their jobs.[29] Occasionally professional "torches," who are frequently members of organized crime, will be hired to set fire to a business. Some businessmen are also driven to deal with gangsters by their search for capital with which to expand their businesses, although others become involved with organized crime without knowing they are doing so. Gangsters often seek to destroy competition and to take over legitimate enterprises, and they frequently use violence to do so. They may also siphon off assets from a legitimate firm for use in such profitable endeavors as drug importation and loan sharking. There is thus some evidence that the drive for profits may lead businessmen into criminal behavior, although studies of OPA violations do not show that they were closely related to the profits or sales of the offending companies.[30]

One study which suggests a connection between profit motivation and violation of the law is Quinney's investigation of prescription violations by pharmacists.[31] He found that pharmacists who had a business orientation rather than a professional orientation toward their job were less bound by occupational norms; they stressed merchandising, inventory turnover, and sales rather than service. Their approach was that of a businessman engaged in the pursuit of profits, whereas other pharmacists were closer to physicians in their orientation. Most importantly, pharmacists with a business orientation had a considerably higher rate of

[27]Willem Bonger, *Criminality and Economic Conditions*, abridged and with an introduction by Austin T. Turk (Bloomington: Indiana University Press, 1916, 1969), pp. 134-37.

[28]Robert E. Lane, *The Regulation of Businessmen: Social Conditions of Government Economic Control* (New Haven: Yale University Press, 1954), p. 94.

[29]William K. Stevens, "Arson Increasing Rapidly; Recession Called a Factor," *The New York Times*, April 13, 1975, pp. 1, 45.

[30]Marshall B. Clinard, *The Black Market: A Study of White Collar Crime* (Montclair, N.J.: Patterson Smith, 1952, 1969), pp. 313-26.

[31]Richard Quinney, "Occupational Structure and Criminal Behavior: Prescription Violations of Retail Pharmacists," *Social Problems*, 11 (Fall 1963), 179-85.

prescription violation than the other pharmacists. This study suggests that the drive for profits may be an important determinant of law-violating behavior even in prosperous times.

One industry in which the profit drive is especially strong is the pharmaceutical industry. If a new drug is approved quickly by the Food and Drug Administration and is well-promoted, large windfall profits are possible through extensive advertising and aggressive salesmanship. Intense competition and a strong drive for profits at times lead to falsification of data on new drugs and to unethical sales techniques to promote them. The Richardson-Merrell pharmaceutical company exemplified this in its promotion of the drug MER/29 during the early 1960s. This anti-cholesterol agent had a number of harmful side effects, including interruption of normal sexual functioning, loss of hair, and eye cataracts. Even after the company learned of these harmful consequences, it issued the following internal memorandum to salesmen:

> When a doctor says your drug causes a side effect, the immediate reply is: "Doctor, what other drug is the patient taking?" Even if you know your drug can cause the side effect mentioned, chances are equally good the same side effect is being caused by a second drug! You let your drug take the blame when you counter with a defensive answer.[32]

Corporate officials vetoed printing a warning on the package that loss of hair might result from the use of the drug, because they felt such a warning would be "rather frightening"; instead, there was a warning about possible "thinning of the hair."[33] Even then, the justification of the warning was to protect the company against possible damage suits rather than to protect the unsuspecting customer. At the same time that the company was gathering concrete information about the negative effects of the drug, it was engaged in an intensified campaign to sell the drug to physicians. The reports which the company had sent to the FDA about MER/29 were later found to contain "smoothed out data," i.e., faked charts on the results of experiments with the drug. Eventually, permission to market the drug was withdrawn by the FDA after numerous reports of harmful consequences had been received. However, the company managed to get in two more days of the hard sell while negotiating

---

[32]Cited in Sanford J. Ungar, "Get Away with What You Can," in Robert L. Heilbroner and others, *In the Name of Profit: Profiles in Corporate Irresponsibility* (Garden City, N.Y.: Doubleday & Co., Inc., 1972), p. 112.

[33]*Ibid.*, p. 114.

with the FDA over the exact wording of the letter it would send to physicians to withdraw the drug from the market. Here we see a company in a highly competitive and highly profitable industry resorting to unethical and probably illegal tactics to sell its product.

The largest loss in a single business crime can also be attributed in part to a desire to create a highly profitable enterprise. The Equity Funding Corporation of America fraud, uncovered in 1973, was a crime which involved an estimated loss of $2 billion. The apparent motive behind this complex fraud was to create a

> good earnings record [which] would increase the value of the stock and thereby enrich the conspirators, who held large amounts of stock and who received more through the years as bonuses. Furthermore, inflated reported earnings and assets made it possible for EFCA to acquire other companies in exchange for its stock and to borrow money with which to make other acquisitions and finance the company's operations which were losing huge amounts each year.[34]

Personal theft played a small part in the fraud; the primary goal of the conspirators was "to make EFCA the largest, fastest growing, most successful financial institution in the world and in the process thereby to gain fame and fortune for themselves."[35] The fact that prestige would be dependent on creating a highly profitable firm indicates the high regard for profit-making in the world of business.

In a free enterprise system, the drive for profits is theoretically tempered by the second element of the system, open competition among firms. In the United States the law prohibits blatant anti-competitive behavior, although in some other societies such as the Soviet Union it is an offense to compete with the state's economic monopolies.[36] In the presence of vague and unenforceable business ethics and ineffective government regulation, competition is pointed to by businessmen as the means by which socially harmful acts are prevented.[37] Ideally, a profitable

[34]Parker, *Crime by Computer,* pp. 120–21.

[35]*Ibid.,* p. 122. In a sidelight to this case, the SEC alleged that five investment advisers and a mutual fund engaged in fraud by using inside information about the Equity Funding scandal to their own advantage. See Richard Phalon, "S.E.C. Says 6 Gained in Equity Fraud Case," *The New York Times,* August 26, 1976, pp. 49, 51.

[36]Hermann Mannheim, *Comparative Criminology* (Boston: Houghton Mifflin Company, 1965), p. 497.

[37]William N. Leonard and Marvin Glenn Weber, "Automakers and Dealers: A Study of Criminogenic Market Forces," *Law and Society Review,* 4 (February 1970), 410.

business activity will attract other businessmen to compete with the innovators in the field, thus reducing profits to a "fair" level. However, competition also stimulates the exploitation of consumers because businessmen may seek to reduce the relative strength of their competitors. The drive for profits is an incentive for businessmen to restrict or eliminate competition; after all, what company which is making a good profit desires the competition which would drive its profits down to a "fair" level? Competition thus often "accelerates diffusion of sharp practices" which enhance profitability.[38]

Sutherland noted that the goal of most businessmen is not to encourage competition, as is suggested by their voiced faith in an unregulated economy, but rather to destroy competition. This goal is often sought through such restraint of trade actions as price-fixing and discriminatory price-cutting. Businessmen may also try to reduce competition by reducing their competitors' sales or by increasing their costs. They may pressure or bribe dealers not to stock a competitor's product. They may try to get banks to charge their competitors higher rates of interest or to deny them credit altogether.[39] They may justify such behavior by citing the need to preserve their own business or to tie production to demand in a predictable way.[40] When competition is suppressed, the public may be "overcharged and undersupplied" and resources may be misallocated, although recent studies suggest that the cost of some monopolized goods does not drop much when free competition is introduced to a market.[41]

One legal way to enhance profitability by reducing competition is the use of patents and copyrights. Other acts restricting competition are illegal and violate antitrust laws; one such act which sometimes leads to criminal prosecution is price-fixing. Another offense designed to provide a company with a competitive advantage is industrial espionage. Profits often depend on gaining a toehold in a new market or on introducing a new product before competitors can develop a similar product. This feat often requires a firm to hide new ideas from competitors. To prevent competitors from profiting through innovation, some firms hire industrial spies to steal information about a new product from other firms or

[38]Elmer Hubert Johnson, *Crime, Correction and Society*, 3rd ed. (Homewood, Ill.: Dorsey Press, 1973), p. 161.

[39]Sutherland, *White Collar Crime*, pp. 76-78.

[40]*Ibid.*, pp. 61, 85-87.

[41]Robert L. Heilbroner, "Controlling the Corporation," in Heilbroner and others, *In the Name of Profit*, pp. 229-31.

to gain access to secrets by hiring their rivals' employees at higher salaries.[42] The law regarding the theft of industrial secrets is somewhat vague, but a burglary to gain information is clearly a violation of the law.

Some corporations have sought to increase their profits and reduce competition in foreign markets through payoffs to government officials and influential citizens. Some of the larger bribes admitted to by American corporations are included in the following chart from *Newsweek* magazine:[43]

Ashland Oil, Inc.	Admits paying more than $300,000 to foreign officials, including $150,000 to President Albert Bernard Bongo of Gabon to retain mineral and refining rights.
Burroughs Corp.	Admits that $1.5 million in corporate funds may have been used in improper payments to foreign officials.
Exxon Corp.	Admits paying $740,000 to government officials and others in three countries. Admits its Italian subsidiary made $27 million in secret but legal contributions to seven Italian political parties.
Gulf Oil Corp.	Admits paying $4 million to South Korea's ruling political party. Admits giving $460,000 to Bolivian officials—including a $110,000 helicopter to the late President René Barrientos Orutño—for oil rights.
Lockheed Aircraft Corp.	Admits giving $202 million in commissions, payoffs and bribes to foreign agents and government officials in the Netherlands, Italy, Japan, Turkey, and other countries. Admits that $22 million of this sum went for outright bribes.
McDonnell Douglas Corp.	Admits paying $2.5 million in commissions and consultant fees between 1970 and 1975 to foreign government officials.
Merck & Co., Inc.	Admits giving $3 million, largely in "commission-type payments," to employees of 36 foreign governments between 1968 and 1975.

[42]Stephen Barlay, *The Secrets Business* (New York: Thomas Y. Crowell Company, 1973).

[43]Larry Martz and others, "Payoffs: The Growing Scandal," *Newsweek,* 87 (February 23, 1976), 30.

Northrop Corp.	Admits in part SEC charges that it paid $30 million in commissions and bribes to government officials and agents in Holland, Iran, France, West Germany, Saudi Arabia, Brazil, Malaysia, and Taiwan.
G. D. Searle & Co.	Admits paying $1.3 million to foreign governmental employees from 1973 to 1975 to "obtain sales of products or services."
United Brands Co.	Admits paying a $1,250,000 bribe to Honduran officials for a reduction in the banana export tax. Admits paying $750,000 to European officials. Investigators say the payment was made to head off proposed Italian restrictions on banana imports.

Some of these bribes were consistent with and supportive of American foreign policy; others were injurious to the interests of the United States abroad.

Businessmen operating in foreign nations argue that "when in Rome, do as the Romans do." They justify bribery as normative and necessary for successful competition with others who engage in similar practices. Bribes help businessmen get favorable tax treatment by foreign governments; this was the apparent motive for the $1.25 million bribe by United Brands Company to the Honduran government. Bribes may also help a company protect its assets abroad, an apparent motive for Gulf Oil Corporation's payoffs to foreign politicians. Bribes allow businessmen to cut red tape, to obtain visas for salespeople, to clear customs, and to prevent delays; when dealing with such highly perishable products as bananas, taking care of such matters may be critical to the maintenance of profits. Bribes may also ease the winning of foreign contracts; Lockheed payoffs helped the company to obtain contracts for new airplanes, and Northrop payoffs to Saudi Arabian generals helped promote the sale of their aircraft. Lobbyists who are foreign nationals may assist a company in this process of competing for contracts, as did the officials whom Lockheed paid in Japan and in the Netherlands. Another motive for bribery is to gain influence over foreign officials by aiding them during elections; Gulf Oil Corporation has done this in South Korea. Exxon Corporation has also made such contributions, including a highly controversial payment to the Communist Party of Italy. Yet another use of bribes is money paid to foreign journalists to plant stories favorable to a company in the press; Lockheed has engaged in this practice.

Businessmen defend foreign bribes as the only way they can do business in certain countries. When bribery is routine, they claim an obligation to pay bribes in order to win contracts for their companies. In one survey of a nonrepresentative sample of 73 businessmen, three-fourths of them said that they had encountered foreign demands for payoffs; nearly half felt that they should pay a bribe if it were a routine practice in the country. Only about one-fourth of the businessmen thought that such payoffs were a problem for their industry. No clear guidelines existed within their companies for dealing with requests for bribes; three-fourths of them said that their company had no written rules for dealing with such situations.[44]

Bribery of foreign officials is not in itself a violation of American laws, although laws against it have been proposed since the extent of such bribery has become public knowledge. Some have recommended criminal penalties for the payment of such bribes, but others favor the strengthening of disclosure requirements. Many of the companies which have paid bribes have violated existing SEC regulations regarding full disclosure, a rule designed to protect stockholders by requiring companies to account fully for their expenditures. Many companies have also violated IRS regulations which allow companies to deduct agents' fees paid for doing business abroad but which do not allow them to deduct bribes which have been paid; the distinction between agents' fees and bribes is not always clear in practice. Bribery may also violate FTC rules regarding fair competition and antitrust activity. Although few American companies have been punished for their involvement in foreign payoffs, foreign officials who have taken such bribes have been dealt with quite harshly. Former Prime Minister Tanaka of Japan has been indicted for taking bribes from Lockheed to help promote the sale of their airplanes. In the Netherlands, Prince Bernhard's links to Lockheed for a time threatened to end the reign of his wife, Queen Juliana; instead, he resigned from all his military and business posts following the release of a government report which found no clear evidence of his taking of bribes but which did criticize his "unacceptable" ties with Lockheed officials.

[44]Michael C. Jensen, "Many U.S. Executives Reported in Favor of Overseas Bribes," *The New York Times,* February 13, 1976, pp. 45, 49.

So restraint of trade, industrial espionage, and foreign bribery are three ways in which businessmen have sought to eliminate or reduce any competition which adversely affects their profits. Competition is acceptable as long as it does not interfere with the profitability of the firm. When businessmen can act to increase their profits without any obvious risk of legal sanction and without incurring public disfavor, which would reduce "goodwill" and harm the firm's competitive position in the marketplace, they sometimes violate the law to do so.

The Market Structure

Crime in the business world is in part a function of market structure, the economic power and leverage available to firms in a particular industrial setting. Today's economy is characterized by weak market and distribution safeguards. Most consumer goods are sold by chain stores and other large organizations with mobile personnel; since business executives are unknown to consumers, there are few checks on abuses. The "essentially faceless transactional environment" at the retail sales level is reflected in such impersonal instrumentalities as credit cards and computers. Such a market situation is conducive to certain types of business crime, including fraudulent advertising and overbilling [45]

Among the market conditions conducive to such business crimes are the following:

1. Seller concentration. If a large share of the market is held by a few leading producers, antitrust violations may occur and false entry barriers may be created. Trade associations may help spread such illegal techniques in concentrated industries.
2. Buyer concentration. A small number of buyers or a great deal of economic wealth in the hands of a few buyers may lead to bribes and kickbacks from sellers.
3. Product differentiation. In distinguishing its product from competing products in the consumer's mind, a company may engage in fraudulent or deceptive advertising to create false distinctions.
4. Entry barriers. Barriers to entry can be created by such practices as discriminatory pricing or dumping in order to drive out competitors in certain locales.

[45]Herbert Edelhertz, *The Nature, Impact and Prosecution of White-Collar Crime* (Washington, D.C.: U.S. Government Printing Office, 1970), p. 5.

5. Price elasticity of demand. When demand is price-inelastic — i.e., when an increase in price will result in little reduction in demand for a good or service — price-fixing may occur.

6. Growth rate of demand. A slow growth rate of demand may encourage false or misleading advertising in order to stimulate consumption and raise profits.[46]

One crime which is directly related to the nature of the market structure is price-fixing. Price-fixing is the exercise of joint economic power through agreement or collusion to raise prices, exclude competitors, and restrict price competition.[47] This offense is particularly common in industries in which the bulk of output is in the hands of a few producers who can easily convene to fix prices, where the demand for the product is price-inelastic, where prices are unstable, and where there are such obstacles to free entry as the need for capital investment, sophisticated technical skills, or patent rights.[48] Firms in industries characterized by intense pressure for profits may seek a "reasonable" division of the market by rigging bids on contracts; this practice raises prices and increases a firm's share of the market.[49] When greater profits can be made through the fixing of prices than through legitimate competition and when the risk of legal sanction is low, favorable conditions for this crime exist; ideological attachment to the notion of open competition then takes second place to the desire for high profits. The fixing of prices may be rationalized as an improvement of a bad market situation. The fact that price-fixing costs consumers money will be ignored or rationalized; executives may claim that they do not wish to hurt consumers and that they personally gain nothing from the price-fixing.

These elements of the market structure were present in the electrical equipment industry prior to the 1961 conviction of 29 companies for price-fixing. These companies controlled 95 percent of the market in electrical goods at the time. There was less price-fixing at times when prices were high and more when prices were low.[50] Erratic short-term

[46]Leonard and Weber, "Automakers and Dealers," pp. 410-11.

[47]A. D. Neale, *The Antitrust Laws of the United States of America* (Cambridge, England: Cambridge University Press, 1970), pp. 32-62.

[48]Leonard and Weber, "Automakers and Dealers," pp. 408-11.

[49]Gilbert Geis, "White Collar Crime: The Heavy Electrical Equipment Antitrust Cases of 1961," in *Criminal Behavior Systems: A Typology,* ed. Marshall B. Clinard and Richard Quinney (New York: Holt, Rinehart and Winston, Inc., 1967), p. 143.

[50]Gilbert Geis, "Victimization Patterns in White-Collar Crime," in *Victimology: A New Focus, Volume 5: Exploiters and Exploited,* ed. Israel Drapkin and Emilio Viano (Lexington, Mass.: D. C. Heath and Company, 1975), p. 91.

fluctuations in prices created a desire to stabilize prices. There was a perceived threat that cutthroat competition would reduce profits to an intolerably low level. Executives felt that consumers would tolerate a rise in the moderate prices for electrical products, especially since the demand for such goods was relatively inelastic.

The American automobile industry is also characterized by elements conducive to certain business crimes. It is highly concentrated in production but diffused in consumption. Cars are sold through local dealerships, which are franchises purchased by local businessmen who have the nonexclusive right to sell and service cars produced by one of the four major manufacturers. Dealers face sales quotas and contests designed to stimulate sales. Minimum stress is placed on service; the Detroit manufacturers regard it as a necessary evil. Dealerships have been canceled for failure to meet sales quotas but not for poor service. Leonard and Weber refer to the auto manufacturers as "socially dangerous persons" because they "cause the causes" of crime by creating pressure to sell new cars but to neglect service to older cars.

There has been an increase in sharp and deceptive service practices by auto dealers in recent years. Reasons for this include an increased number of cars on the road, a lower number of mechanics in proportion to the number of cars, and more complex cars of which the owners are ignorant. These factors, and the pressure to de-emphasize service in favor of new sales, have led to considerable service gouging; examples include overcharging for labor and parts, unnecessary work, and the use of rebuilt parts which are charged as new parts. Similar practices occur in auto repair shops which are not connected to car dealerships; one recent study found that only eleven of twenty-four shops in the New York City area passed a test of honesty. Two completely misdiagnosed a simple problem and eleven performed costly work which was unnecessary. Dishonesty was not related to the type of shop, its size, its site, or its volume of business.[51]

For dealer repairs which are covered by warranty, auto manufacturers set standard amounts of time that those repairs should take. This system induces mechanics to beat those times by doing superficial work, using new parts rather than taking the time to repair old ones, and allowing little time for diagnosis. Since dealers are reimbursed only a standard amount for a particular job covered by warranty, there is pressure to cut corners to get work done within the allotted time. Warranties also con-

[51]Frances Cerra, "Auto-Repair Problems: Causes and Some Safeguards," *The New York Times,* December 9, 1975, pp. 39, 46.

tribute to illegal or unethical behavior in another way. With increased warranty coverage during the 1960s, more defective cars were delivered to dealers as manufacturers increasingly placed responsibility on them for preparing cars for sale. Since the manufacturers' labor rates for warranty work were so low and since some repairs were disallowed after they had been made, dealers sometimes tried to convince owners that certain work was not covered by warranty or that their cars would have to be left for several days to take care of the problem, thereby discouraging owners from having repairs made. One manufacturer even sponsored a contest among dealers to see which one could underspend his warranty budget by the greatest amount.

One factor which affects the market structure of an industry is government regulation. Regulations may be conducive to bribery, kickbacks, and payoffs. For instance, the Knapp Commission Report of Police Corruption in New York City found that police regulation of the construction industry was a "serious corruption hazard."[52] Bribes were necessary to get anything done in the "maze of City ordinances and regulations."[53] Paying bribes was less expensive than obeying the law, although bribes may add as much as 1 or 2 percent to the cost of all building construction in New York City.[54] To erect a building in New York, it was necessary to secure between 40 and 130 different permits and licenses. The rules were generally viewed as "nuisances which interfere with efficient construction work"; as a result, large companies often used an "expeditor" to handle payoffs to the police, inspectors, and city clerks.[55] It was also frequently necessary to pay off union representatives and union workers in order to get work done on time and to avoid costly delays. That corruption "is a fact of life in the construction industry" was made clear in a survey of 95 city workers who had contact with the industry; all of them were either personally involved in the corruption or knew of it.[56] A city building inspector earning $11,000 a year could collect as much as an extra $10,000 to $30,000 a year in bribes. Thus

[52]*The Knapp Commission Report on Police Corruption* (New York: George Braziller, 1972), p. 19.

[53]*Ibid.*, p. 68.

[54]David K. Shipler, "Study Finds $25-Million Yearly in Bribes Is Paid by City's Construction Industry," *The New York Times*, June 26, 1972, pp. 1, 26.

[55]*Knapp Commission Report*, p. 125.

[56]*Ibid.*, p. 124; Edward Ranzal, "City Report Finds Building Industry Infested by Graft," *The New York Times*, November 8, 1974, pp. 1, 48.

inspectors and others were willing to overlook infractions in return for payoffs, and construction companies were willing to pay the money to avoid the complex web of city regulations.

OPA regulations during and after World War II were responsible for generating a black market, since unfilled consumer demand created a pressure to violate price ceilings and rationing controls. Hidden price increases took the form of overceiling charges, cash payments in addition to recorded ones, tying-in agreements under which consumers bought unwanted products in order to obtain wanted ones, short-weighting, and grading violations. Black market violations were most common in industries which were loosely organized and relatively unstructured.[57] For example, between 1939 and 1946 the number of meatpackers in the United States rose from 1,492 to 26,660. Given the decentralized nature of the enterprise and the high demand for meat among consumers, one would expect high rates of violations. Surveys found that between 77 and 94 percent of the retail meat stores which were supplied by the meatpackers were violating OPA ceiling prices; as much as two-thirds of the meat sold under the OPA regulations was sold on the black market.[58]

Bribery and payoffs also exist in today's meatpacking industry.[59] Department of Agriculture inspectors exercise considerable discretion in their enforcement of regulations. Sometimes they are given overtime work by the packers they are supposedly controlling; occasionally they receive gifts and favors from them. The inspectors sometimes justify these gifts by distinguishing in their own minds between gratuities (which they feel are acceptable) and bribes (which they feel are unacceptable), although federal law prohibits them from accepting any money or gifts from companies they are inspecting. Although it is also illegal for a company to offer anything to an inspector, it is usually the inspector who is punished when cases of bribery come to light.[60]

Regulations controlling the inspection and shipping of grain have also been violated with regularity. In this instance, inspectors are private individuals who are licensed by the Department of Agriculture. Since

[57]Walter C. Reckless, *The Crime Problem,* 5th ed. (New York: Appleton-Century-Crofts, 1973), p. 324.

[58]"The Boom," *Fortune,* 33 (June 1946), 257.

[59]Jonathan Kwitny, " 'Necessary' Payoffs — But Who Really Pays?" in *Swindled! Classic Business Frauds of the Seventies,* ed. Donald Moffitt (Princeton, N.J.: Dow Jones Books, 1976), pp. 127-55.

[60]Peter Schuck, "The Curious Case of the Indicted Meat Inspectors," *Harper's Magazine,* 245 (September 1972), 81-88.

the income of grain companies depends on the amount of grain shipped and the speed with which it can be dispatched, there is pressure on the inspectors to overlook violations. Indeed, it is often easier and cheaper for the grain company to bribe an inspector than it is to clean the ship and properly label the grain. In 1975 a number of inspectors were indicted and pleaded guilty to taking bribes to certify ships fit for the shipment of grain.[61]

Domestic regulations have been avoided by some businessmen through the use of the international market. Just as the lack of laws governing interstate behavior such as the fraudulent advertisement of land makes prosecution of such offenses difficult, so the unregulated nature of the international economy often allows businessmen to avoid legal sanctions which would follow from similar behavior within the United States. The use of Swiss banks to "launder" money from the United States is one example of the exploitation of the unregulated international market to violate domestic laws with impunity. This method has been used to evade tax payments, to reinvest funds controlled by organized crime, and to make illegal campaign contributions. Another example of the use of the international vacuum in regulations is the criminal activities of Bernard Cornfeld and later Robert Vesco within Investors Overseas Services, an offshore investment company. "By working, so to speak, in the interstices between the world's jurisdictions and administrative systems, they were able to do with impunity things that would have been illegal had their enterprise been located in any one place."[62]

Trust and Credit

Business transactions in the United States often depend on trust. Trust, however, is also conducive to certain business crimes; one scholar has even defined white collar crime as "a breach of a fiduciary duty sufficient to warrant the intervention of society."[63] Such an offense may

---

[61]William Robbins, "U.S. Agents Push a Broad Inquiry into Grain Trade," *The New York Times*, May 20, 1975, pp. 1, 25.

[62]C. Raw, B. Page, and G. Hodgson, cited in John A. Mack, in collaboration with Hans-Jürgen Kerner, *The Crime Industry* (Westmead, England: Saxon House, D.C. Heath Ltd., 1975), p. 22.

[63]William N. Hannay, "Introduction" to a Symposium on White-Collar Crime, *The American Criminal Law Review*, 11 (Summer 1973), 819.

occur when businessmen hold "two or more incompatible and conflicting positions of trust."[64] Also, with increasing affluence there has been a growth in the number of opportunities available for the violation of fiduciary trust, including estates, union and company pension funds, welfare benefits, mutual funds, and credit unions.[65]

Trust is necessary for the smooth functioning of the commercial world. However, it may be abused by one party to an economic relationship, whether it be a business partner as in Vesco's exploitation of his colleagues in IOS, a worker who steals from his employer, an author such as Clifford Irving or Chief Red Fox who submits a fraudulent or plagiarized manuscript as his own work, an employer who engages in illegal labor practices, or corporate directors who deceive investors through failure to disclose information.

The Equity Funding Corporation of America violated the trust upon which the insurance industry operates through its resale at discount of insurance policies written on nonexistent clients. According to the Trustee's Bankruptcy Report,

> only someone with an exceedingly skeptical bent of mind would have . . . inferred fraud. Such an inference would have been hostile to the presumption of good faith and honest-dealing which customarily prevails in American business practice. To the Trustee, that presumption, though sometimes grievously abused, is probably indispensable to a vigorous and productive economy.[66]

Trust was reinforced in this particular crime through the use of the computer to print out insurance policies; the common assumption that anything which comes out of a computer must be correct was an important element in the deception. Trust of the stockholders in the company was also violated through the manipulation of assets to suggest a higher degree of profitability than was the case.

In the financial world, faith in a businessman is based in large part on the image projected by the individual. Proper dress, manners, and bearing are taken as signs of trustworthiness and integrity. However, a dishonest businessman may intentionally create a front in order to exploit this superficial way of judging one's reliability. A variation is to

[64] Edwin H. Sutherland, "Crime and Business," *The Annals of the American Academy of Political and Social Science,* 217 (September 1941), 112.

[65] Edelhertz, *Nature, Impact and Prosecution,* p. 6.

[66] Cited in Parker, *Crime by Computer,* p. 166.

maintain secrecy for oneself and thus prevent others from assessing one's character. Usually this alternative is available only to those who have already established considerable economic power. This technique was used by Ivar Kreuger, the perpetrator of one of the largest swindles in history. Kreuger demanded absolute secrecy for his transactions and thus prevented those with whom he dealt from checking up on him. He was responsible for financial swindles which caused "probably the greatest blow the morale of the world of finance as a whole has ever suffered."[67]

Another type of trust abuse is labor racketeering, "the abuse of an individual's position in the labor field for his personal enrichment and at the expense of workers or employers in industry or both."[68] Labor racketeering may involve collusion with managers against their competitors, depriving union members of their rights, theft of union funds, nepotism in hiring practices, kickbacks, or "sweetheart contracts" (a management bribe for labor peace).[69]

Trust is also abused in the solicitation of funds for nonexistent charities. An estimated $100 million a year is collected by such charity rackets; this is nearly half as much as all endowed foundations spend each year.[70] There may be as many as ten charity frauds for every legitimate charity.[71] Such fraudulent appeals often involve a sales pitch by telephone and then the dispatch of a messenger to pick up the donation. Another technique is the unauthorized mailing of articles with a request for a donation to pay for the goods. Charity frauds involve misrepresentation of the intent of the fund-raising effort, the unauthorized use of endorsements by public figures, the diversion of funds, and excessive operating costs. Charity frauds undermine public trust in legitimate charities and make the job of fund-raising by legitimate groups more difficult.[72]

[67]Robert Shaplen, *Kreuger: Genius and Swindler* (New York: Alfred A. Knopf, 1960), p. 230.

[68]J. F. Bell, "Corruption and Union Racketeering," *Current History,* 36 (June 1959), 343.

[69]*Ibid.*

[70]Frank E. Andrews, *Philanthropic Giving* (New York: Russell Sage Foundation, 1950), pp. 160-71.

[71]H. H. Buck, "Charity Appeals," *Editorial Research Reports,* September 11, 1953, pp. 629-45.

[72]Scott M. Cutlip, *Fund-Raising in the United States: Its Role in America's Philanthropy* (New Brunswick, N.J.: Rutgers University Press, 1965), pp. 441-76.

Merchants sometimes abuse the trust which customers place in them through the bait-and-switch technique, misrepresentation of prices, substitution of inferior goods upon delivery, deceptive credit practices, and high markups on inferior goods. These practices occur because the consumer-seller relationship is based on consumer trust of the merchant rather than on skepticism and questioning of every stage of the transaction.

Trust is also abused in the sale of land, which may be sold sight unseen through glossy brochures and promises of development. Advertisements may be fraudulent or merely deceptive, overstating the closeness of natural attractions and exaggerating the desirability of the land.

Another context in which trust relationships are violated is the embezzlement of funds. Cressey concluded from his study of incarcerated trust violators that embezzlement could not be eliminated from the American economic system through better controls over workers or through more regular audits, because trust was essential to the functioning of business; as long as relationships of trust existed, the opportunity to embezzle would be present.[73] A contradictory view is that of Norman Jaspan, a consultant to business on the matter of employee theft. He suggests that workers come to their jobs honest and become thieves because poor supervision creates opportunities for theft. Jaspan proposes that employers should distrust their workers in order to reduce employee theft; he fails to see that the elimination of trust would seriously impede the functioning of most business enterprises.[74]

One trust relationship which is essential to the American economy is credit, which is based on the creditor's faith in the repayment of the debt by the borrower. Credit is necessary to the economic growth of the country; it is also a convenience for consumers, a way to meet needs, and a means to improve a standard of living. Since World War II there has been a substantial expansion in consumer credit; in the two decades after the war, consumer credit increased twelvefold while disposable income increased only threefold.[75] This expansion of credit has created a number of opportunities for criminal behavior. The extension of

[73]Cressey, *Other People's Money.*

[74]Norman Jaspan and Hillel Black, *The Thief in the White Collar* (Philadelphia: J. B. Lippincott Company, 1960); Norman Jaspan, *Mind Your Own Business* (Englewood Cliffs, N.J.: Prentice-Hall, Inc., 1974).

[75]"Translating Sympathy for Deceived Consumers into Effective Programs for Protection," *University of Pennsylvania Law Review,* 114 (January 1966), 410-11.

credit to relatively poor and unsophisticated consumers has opened the way for credit fraud and default on payments. Competition among merchants may sometimes take the form of false or deceptive advertising of "easy" credit terms for customers. Banks show excessive trust in granting credit at times. For example, one man was able to borrow over $732,000 from a bank without any security; he supplied a verbal and written statement of his personal net worth but provided no evidence or collateral to support his statement.[76]

Businessmen seeking to erect financial empires may abuse trust in securing credit. For example, Tony de Angelis borrowed millions of dollars by using nonexistent salad oil as collateral for his loans. He had previously been involved in financial difficulties, but none of his creditors checked on his past, just as none of them checked to see whether the empty tanks were actually filled with salad oil. The ease with which credit was granted made his massive fraud possible. Although the effect of this fraud on the stock market and the commodities market was significant, the financiers were primarily concerned with recovery of their losses; they showed little interest in learning how they had been swindled or how to prevent a recurrence of the situation. Although the financiers had not violated the law, their trust of "a respected member of the business community" and their willingness to grant him credit were essential to the perpetration of the crime.[77] Another case of abuse of credit by a businessman seeking to build a financial empire was that of Frank W. Sharp, a Texan who created "a large and tangled business empire" through indebtedness and borrowing.[78] Sharp also relied on a good public image which he developed through such activities as donations to local charities, and he facilitated his violation of the law through bribery of public officials. Both de Angelis and Sharp illustrate the claim that the way to wealth in the United States is through massive indebtedness, although both violated the law in the process of creating their financial power.

The credit economy has also spawned the crime of bankruptcy fraud. Willem Bonger recognized 60 years ago that some businesses were

[76]Dena Kleiman, "How a Man Bilked Chase of $732,000 by Duping Banker," *The New York Times,* April 25, 1976, pp. 1, 49.

[77]Norman C. Miller, *The Great Salad Oil Swindle* (New York: Coward-McCann, 1965), p. 11.

[78]A. James Reichley, "The Texas Banker Who Bought Politicians," *Fortune,* 84 (December 1971), 94-99, 143-46.

knowingly established in order to fail, with the founders profiting from failure through stock dealings.[79] A related business crime is the "scam."[80] In this bankruptcy fraud, racketeers purchase a business with a good credit rating, or they establish a front business, often with a name very similar to an existing business which is respected by the public. The racketeers then stock up on merchandise which they purchase on credit, often with money supplied by organized crime. They commonly deal in merchandise which has broad consumer appeal, can be bought in volume, is easy to transport and hard to trace, and can be quickly converted into cash; office equipment, electrical appliances, televisions, hi-fi sets, jewelry, and toys meet these requirements. They demand quick delivery, pay for the first orders on arrival so as to establish good credit and then buy to the limit on credit, attributing their nonpayment to the rapid expansion of their business. (Scams often occur at Christmas time, when suppliers are too busy to do a thorough credit check or to demand prompt payment of bills.) The next step is to sell the goods as quickly as possible through discount outlets or by direct mail and then abandon their empty stores, leaving their creditors with unpaid bills. Often they are then forced into involuntary bankruptcy by their creditors, but this step has little significance for them once they have made their money.

Another abuse of the credit system is misuse of the holder in due course, which one judge has called "the mask behind which fraud hides."[81] This involves the sale of a merchant's contract to a financial institution at a discount; the financial agency then collects installment payments from the customer and is able to make a profit when the cost of the product and the interest payments are paid in full. The merchant uses the cash, which is made immediately available, to replenish his stock. This system has been the source of widespread abuse, since the customer is left with no recourse if he finds the merchandise he has bought is defective. The merchant tells the customer that a financial institution now owns the contract and that he has been absolved of any responsibility regarding the merchandise. The financial institution tells the consumer that it did not sell the merchandise and bears no responsibility for the customer's transaction with the merchant. The Federal Trade Commission tried

---

[79]Bonger, *Criminality and Economic Conditions,* pp. 139-41.

[80]Edward J. DeFranco, *Anatomy of a Scam: A Case Study of a Planned Bankruptcy by Organized Crime* (Washington, D.C.: U.S. Government Printing Office, 1973).

[81]Cited in "Translating Sympathy," p. 414.

to assist bewildered consumers in 1975 by ruling that any holder of a consumer credit contract was subject to the debtor's claims against the original merchant and assumed his obligations when it purchased the contract.[82] What effect this extension of liability to financial institutions will have cannot yet be determined.

Recently there has been an increase in yet another abuse of the credit system. Theft and fraudulent use of credit cards have become major problems as consumer credit has expanded. Consumers have also been victimized by companies which engage in false billing of customers in the hope that bills will be paid without question; the use of computerized statements adds an aura of infallibility to the billing system.

Hans Georg Ansel has argued that since money is an anonymous but legally approved claim on the economic system and its resources and since it has liquidity, it is the source of most crimes against property.[83] He claims that a computerized system of accounts which eliminated most cash flow would thus reduce crime. However, a cashless society in which most transactions were done by crediting and debiting accounts stored in computers might merely increase the number of computer crimes, a costly type of offense which has been increasing in recent years.

Computers have also been suggested as a solution to another type of crime, the theft of stocks and bonds. If possession of a paper certificate were replaced by information stored in a computer, and if transfers of stocks were made over communication circuits between computers, some theft of certificates might be eliminated, although new forms of theft through manipulation of computerized accounts would probably develop. Stock theft became a serious problem during the period from 1966 to 1968, when rapid expansion of the securities industry increased the number of sales facilities and branch offices and the amount of paperwork. Record-keeping machinery and the system for the delivery and transfer of securities became clogged; locating the actual paper certificates became difficult. The expansion of business meant an influx of new, low-paid workers. This led to increased theft as organized crime succeeded in planting employees in some of the expanding firms because of inadequate attention to the background of new employees; at other times, organized crime used employees who were indebted to bookies or

---

[82]Diane Henry, "F.T.C. Strengthens Rights of Buyers," *The New York Times,* May 15, 1975, pp. 1, 33.

[83]Hans Georg Ansel, "Money and Criminality: A Reorientation of Criminological Research," *International Journal of Criminology and Penology,* 1 (May 1973), 179–87.

loan sharks to steal securities. Although the gangsters did not control the brokerage houses, they were able to have securities stolen and they then fenced these securities. Often they used the stolen stocks and bonds as collateral for loans; certificates were rarely checked by banks as long as the debtor continued to pay the interest on his loan.

The market structure of the securities industry is also conducive to the theft of stocks and bonds. First, the paper certificate itself can be stolen, counterfeited, or used fraudulently; this is possible because of the emphasis on sales and promotion and the lag in paperwork in the industry. Second, the massive volume of separate transactions makes it difficult to check all traded certificates against a list of stolen ones. Brokerage houses generally oppose a national clearinghouse to check securities against a "hot list" because of the cost and inconvenience of such a system and because they fear that it would hamper sales. They are willing to sustain some theft if the cost of eliminating that theft is the disruption of sales. Third, effective control is difficult because of the lack of international administration of the securities industry and because of the frequent use of foreign banks, especially by gangsters. Fourth, the cornerstone of the modern securities industry is the concept of the "bona fide purchaser"; "under normal business transactions, a bona fide purchaser takes possession free of claims from their former owners—even if they are stolen securities."[84] Banks which borrow or loan money against stolen securities legally own the stocks if they exercised "due diligence" prior to the transaction's completion.[85]

The suggestion to reduce the theft of certificates through computerization of stock transactions has been opposed by those in the industry as potentially disruptive of trade. Computerized central records would also give a potential criminal access to a massive amount of information which he could manipulate for his own purposes. In the absence of written records, computer crimes often are discovered only by accident, as when a computer breaks down or a hand calculation reveals missing funds. Directors and executives of corporations usually lack the necessary skills to determine if a computer crime has been committed, and even systematic audits may fail to turn up evidence of a crime.

Stock manipulation and theft is only one of a large number of computer crimes which might become more common with the increasing

[84]Matthew G. Yeager, "The Gangster as White Collar Criminal: Organized Crime and Stolen Securities," *Issues in Criminology*, 8 (Spring 1973), 63.

[85]Cole, "How Crime Is Infiltrating," pp. 1, 11.

computerization of business transactions. Donn Parker at the Stanford Research Institute is one of the few investigators who has undertaken a systematic study of the problem of crime by computer.[86] He found that offenders are usually amateur rather than professional thieves. They are usually young (18 to 30 years old) males. They have both the specialized skills necessary to use the computer and easy access to computer facilities. Computer criminals often plan their crimes in detail and require the collusion of other workers to carry out their schemes. Their crimes vary in nature; some steal computer programs and others instruct computers to ignore overdrafts on bank accounts. Others have computers credit money to personal accounts, so it can be seen that the expansion of a cashless economy can increase this type of theft even if it reduces robbery and larceny. Most computer thieves faced nonshareable financial problems which they tried to solve through the manipulation and diversion of funds, although others were most interested in beating a "foolproof" system or in gaining wealth. Parker suggests that computer crime may be reduced through more attention to security, especially by maintaining control over access to computer facilities. Screening potential workers and separating job functions may also reduce such crime, although Parker's data suggest that any weak link in the system will be exploited by a computer specialist with a desire to commit a crime.

The Corporate Structure

Much business crime in the United States takes place in the context of the corporation, an institution which is characterized by large size, bureaucratic structure, impersonality, and rational decision-making. These aspects of the corporation facilitate certain types of business crime.

The large size of the corporation fragments personal responsibility by diffusing it; it is thus difficult to pinpoint exactly who made a particular decision. Supervisors may take responsibility for the successes of their subordinates, but they generally will not admit that they delegated duties to a worker who violates the law.[87] Supervisors may blame underlings for violations of the law, even when their own orders clearly indicated that it would be necessary to violate the law to achieve a goal; business

---

[86]Parker, *Crime by Computer.*

[87]For an interesting fictional account of the evasion of responsibility for criminal actions, see Paul E. Erdman, *The Silver Bears* (New York: Charles Scribner's Sons, 1974).

crime in such cases may then be attributed to a breakdown in communication or to the immorality of the younger generation. The delegation of responsibility and unwritten orders keep those at the top of the corporate structure remote from the consequences of their decisions and orders, much as the heads of organized crime families remain "untouchable" by the law. It is not clear when a corporate officer can speak for the corporation as a legal entity and when he can delegate authority to others; "in the bewildering complexity and intricate ramifications of the administrative set-up in the modern 'big business' corporation, the spheres of delegated authority and of managerial discretion are virtually impossible to disentangle."[88]

In the large corporation the division of tasks is often necessary. Although this enhances the efficiency of the bureaucracy, it also makes control of all business activities problematic. Specialization may contribute to violation of the law if the corporation employs such specialists as accountants and lawyers to tell corporate managers how much they may get away with. Stanley Sporkin, head of the Enforcement Division of the Securities and Exchange Commission, has said that when he worked for a Washington law firm before coming to the SEC, he found it "very disturbing when clients weren't satisfied until they had one leg over the line between right and wrong. We'd tell a client that something was *wrong,* and then he'd ask, *'But is it legal?'* "[89]

Specialization may also be conducive to the violation of the law because of poor communication among departments and lack of effective supervision. The Equity Funding scandal was in part a result of the "Balkanized corporate structure" of the company, which allowed some of the conspirators to lie to other department managers about their fraudulent activities.[90] Also, the decentralization of General Electric in 1950 broke the company into a number of autonomous divisions, each of which was pressured to show a profit; this led to price-fixing as one way to achieve stable prices and predictable profits.

Large corporations may encounter greater problems in supervising subordinates than do smaller corporations. This might produce more

---

[88]Myron W. Watkins, "Electrical Equipment Antitrust Cases: Their Implications for Government and Business," *University of Chicago Law Review,* 29 (August 1961), 107.

[89]Cited in Louis M. Kohlmeier, "The Bribe Busters," *The New York Times Magazine,* September 26, 1976, p. 53.

[90]Raymond L. Dirks and Leonard Gross, *The Great Wall Street Scandal* (New York: McGraw-Hill Book Company, 1974), p. 240.

violation of the law by large corporations. However, Clinard found no clear relationship between the size of a firm and the likelihood of its having violated an OPA regulation.[91] In a study of government regulation of businessmen, Lane hypothesized that larger firms might be less apt to violate the law than smaller ones because they were more likely to hire legal counsel to help them understand the law; however, he found no relationship between size of the firm and the frequency of violation of the law.[92] A survey of 106 firms and their responses to the 1961 price-fixing case found that larger firms were more apt than smaller ones to have large legal staffs and specific programs to prevent antitrust violations; whether these factors affected the frequency of such violations by large firms is uncertain.[93]

There is some evidence that large size may be conducive to certain types of business crime. A 1941 study of car and radio repair shops found that dishonesty was more common when the customer and the owners of the shop were more remote from each other, i.e., cheating was more common in large shops which catered to hotel guests, in independent shops rather than in those tied to car dealerships, and in shops located in larger cities.[94] This study suggests that large shops may be more likely to cheat customers because of the greater anonymity of customer-owner relationships. Another piece of evidence suggesting a link between the size of a firm and violation of the law comes from a study of the filing of erroneous tax returns. The following shows the percentages of firms of varying sizes which filed such returns, with no distinction being made between willful violations and violations due to misunderstanding:

Firms with less than $50,000 in assets	23%
Firms with between $50,000 and $100,000 in assets	33%
Firms with between $100,000 and $250,000 in assets	38%
Firms with between $250,000 and $500,000 in assets	45%
Firms with between $500,000 and $1,000,000 in assets	49%

[91]Clinard, *The Black Market*, p. 325.

[92]Lane, *Regulation of Businessmen*, pp. 97–98.

[93]Richard A. Whiting, "Antitrust and the Corporate Executive II," *Virginia Law Review*, 48 (January 1962), 2.

[94]Roger William Riis and John Patric, *Repairmen Will Get You If You Don't Watch Out* (New York: Doubleday, Doran and Co., Inc., 1942).

These figures indicate that among a group of companies with less than $1 million in assets, the rate of filing an erroneous tax return increased steadily with the size of the firm. Cheating also varied significantly with the industry of the firm; there was the least cheating in real estate and finance and the most among plumbers and contractors. These findings are based on a sample of about 16,000 firms out of a million such firms in the nation.[95]

Large corporations are often highly impersonal institutions. Impersonality may be tied to violation of the law, for workers may feel little loyalty to the institution. Some observers have suggested that "the impersonal nature of the centrally controlled economy" of the Soviet Union is responsible for widespread economic crimes such as graft and embezzlement in that country.[96] However, the large corporations in Western nations create a similar impersonal climate which may facilitate crimes against the firm by workers. The impersonality and increased size which result from corporate mergers may also reduce loyalty to the new corporation, especially among those who feel they are worse off in the new company than in their old firm.[97] The lack of close attachment of workers to their employers may also result from a high rate of job mobility. In a nation such as Japan, where until recently workers were usually tied to one company for life, both by personal choice and by tradition, offenses against the company such as employee theft and embezzlement are probably less common than in nations such as the United States where job mobility is greater. Also, in nations with a tradition of union-management conflict, such as the United States, employee crime against the corporation may be more common because of an attitude that the corporation provides benefits to workers only because of threat and coercion rather than out of sincere concern for their welfare. This feeling may create a climate of resentment and a desire to get back at the company in whatever way possible.

Disgruntled workers often rationalize theft by saying that they are underpaid or abused by their employer.[98] Executives who are frustrated by lack of promotion or salary increments may justify theft or embezzle-

[95]Eileen Shanahan, "Tax Errors Seen among Concerns," *The New York Times*, July 21, 1975, pp. 31-32.

[96]Christopher S. Wren, "Graft and Embezzlement, Most Persistent Crimes in Soviet, Continue to Plague the Economy," *The New York Times*, April 13, 1976, p. 17.

[97]Jaspan, *Mind Your Own Business*, p. 205.

[98]Cressey, *Other People's Money*, pp. 57-66.

ment as a deserved fringe benefit or as compensation for unsatisfactory working conditions. Jaspan suggests that employee theft may be reduced by enhancing job satisfaction, by paying workers more, and by attending to their personal problems.[99] He asserts that workers violate the law to augment their salaries and that the best solution to the problem is to undercut their need for money. However, Zeitlin concludes from a study of 32 workers discharged from a Midwestern clothing store that theft serves functions other than a simple augmentation of income; workers steal to a large extent for job enrichment.[100] Many jobs are repetitive and dull; they provide little opportunity for advancement, little freedom of action, poor pay, high turnover, and little real satisfaction. Of the 32 discharged workers, 8 said they stole for money alone, 6 stole on impulse, and 18 stole for the satisfaction of getting away with it. They felt no guilt since they thought the store could afford the loss. They often blamed working conditions, especially the boring nature of the work and the low pay. They thus stole to get back at the system and to make their jobs more interesting and challenging. Theft for challenge was also found in almost every case of computer crime examined by Parker.[101] In another case, a wealthy man with a law degree allegedly stole $607,000 in bonds because he was "fascinated by the challenge of constructing elaborate schemes to steal money."[102]

Businesses may tolerate or even encourage their workers to steal. A case recounted in Elliot Liebow's *Tally's Corner* indicates that some employers carefully calculate the cost of an employee's theft and adjust his wages accordingly, reducing wages to the level necessary to balance losses through theft. However, this system penalizes the nonthieving worker, and it may lead to punishment for the thieving worker if his employer catches him.[103] Still, theft by a worker may make his job more interesting; indeed, Zeitlin suggests that employers allow a certain amount of theft for this very reason, a position contrary to Jaspan's view that wages should be raised to undercut the need to steal.

[99]Jaspan, *Mind Your Own Business*, pp. 61–80, 93–104.

[100]Lawrence R. Zeitlin, "A Little Larceny Can Do a Lot for Employee Morale," *Psychology Today*, 5 (June 1971), 22–26, 64.

[101]Parker, *Crime by Computer*, pp. 45–47.

[102]Deirdre Carmody, "Law Graduate Held in $607,000," *The New York Times*, February 20, 1974, pp. 1, 45.

[103]Elliot Liebow, *Tally's Corner: A Study of Negro Streetcorner Men* (Boston: Little, Brown and Company, 1967), pp. 37–38.

The modern corporation is a decision-making machine based on rationality. When violations of the law are regular practices of the corporation, they are sometimes the result of a rational assessment of the risks and benefits of engaging in a particular type of behavior; "[t]he psychology of rational choice may be correctly applied to some types of crime, for example white collar crime and organized crime, while for other types it seems wide of the mark."[104] Behavior which violates a law may be engaged in if the risk of apprehension or conviction is thought to be low, if victims are unlikely to complain, if proof of the act is difficult to secure, or if the case can be fixed. Some decisions to violate the law appear to be based on organized and deliberate planning, such as Richardson-Merrell's decision to market MER/29 up to the time the FDA forced them to withdraw the drug from the market even though the company was well aware of the dangers involved in continuing use of the drug. The extent of rationality in corporate decision-making has been questioned by some scholars. For example, Christopher Stone has suggested that a rational calculation to maximize the position of certain key individuals within the firm may be incompatible with a rational calculation to maximize corporate profits. The salaries of certain individuals within the firm may not suffer even if the corporation as a whole is fined for a violation, so rationality may lead them to violate the law even if it is costly to the firm to do so. Also, rational decision-making may be prevented because the flow of information in the corporation is inadequate; indeed, certain laws may impede the free flow of information to top executives as a way of protecting them from knowing that the law is being violated.[105]

Corporate production deadlines and quotas may also contribute to certain business crimes. Quantitative incentives for advancement and salary increase may force workers to compromise their values. One survey found that about two-thirds of a group of 240 businessmen felt pressure to achieve corporate goals by violating their personal standards; four of every five could imagine a situation in which managers were ethical but so demanding of results as to force subordinates to compromise personal standards.[106] Financial incentives may also lead to violation of the law in

[104]Johanaes Andenaes, "General Prevention Revisited: Research and Policy Implications," *Journal of Criminal Law and Criminology*, 66 (September 1975), 340.

[105]Stone, *Where the Law Ends*, pp. 45–46.

[106]William E. Blundell, "Equity Funding: 'I Did It for the Jollies,' " in Moffitt, *Swindled!* p. 88.

order to continue to supplement one's income after the incentives no
longer exist. Job expectations may also push workers to violate the law.
The pressure on workers to complete the production of brakes for an
airplane led them to falsify test results on the performance of the brakes.
Because much money had already been invested in the project, because
the workers were unwilling to risk criticizing their superiors who were
responsible for the faulty brake design, and because the company was
reluctant to admit its failure to the government contractor, a false report
was issued.[107]

The control of information within the corporation is another factor
which is sometimes linked to the violation of the law. Corporate managers
may use information on the financial state of the corporation to their
personal advantage, at the expense of stockholders who do not have the
same information. For this reason, all trading of stock by insiders must
be reported to the Securities and Exchange Commission, although there
is no requirement that stockholders be notified of this directly. The
Equity Funding case involved the manipulation of corporate assets and
the falsification of records which created a public image of a strong
corporation, although the managers were aware of the weakness of the
firm and the overinflated value of its stock. Inside information may be
used for speculation, especially in firms engaged in unstable markets
where such information allows for the prediction of future trends. Other
illegal acts which result from the control of information about the
financial state of the corporation include the purchase or sale of stocks
as a result of information which is not available to the investing public,
concealment of information from stockholders on a matter requiring
their vote, misrepresentation of facts to directors or to stockholders,
leaving corporate interests undefended against outside predators, and
borrowing money to buy stock beyond the limits of margin requirements.[108]

Because business crime is a complex problem on which little empirical
research has been done, the exact causes of such behavior cannot be
specified. However, some conditions which facilitate such crime have
been identified in this chapter. Certain predictive statements can be
made from knowledge of these facilitating conditions, although the

---

[107]Kermit Vandiver, " 'Why Should My Conscience Bother Me?' " in Heilbroner and
others, *In the Name of Profit*, pp. 3–31.

[108]James Boyd, "Men of Distinction," in Heilbroner and others, *In the Name of Profit*,
p. 156.

statements are only tentative. For example, it is possible to predict that markets with a concentration of producers are apt to have more price-fixing violations than markets with a greater diffusion of producers. Empirical testing of such predictive statements will provide greater information on the specific causes of crime in the business world.

four

The Psychology and Sociology of Business Crime

Economic conditions may explain the level of business crime in a society or the variations in crime rates by industry, but they do not explain why particular individuals engage in business crimes while others do not. For such an explanation, one must turn to psychological and sociological approaches. Unfortunately, relatively little empirical research or theoretical work has been done on the psychological and social differences between offenders and nonoffenders in the business world.

Edwin H. Sutherland states that white collar crime cannot be explained by poverty, social and psychological pathologies, low intelligence, or social class.[1] He argues against the usefulness of personality variables in explaining white collar crime, claiming that such crime is ubiquitous in the business world. He also asserts that white collar crime is not rooted in childhood experiences. Sutherland provides no evidence to support these contentions; he collected no data on the personalities of businessmen in his study of white collar crime.

Donald R. Cressey, a student of Sutherland's, concludes from his study of trust violators that embezzlers are not characterized by social and psychological pathologies or by moral weakness, as is commonly

[1]Edwin H. Sutherland, *White Collar Crime* (New York: Holt, Rinehart and Winston, 1949, 1961), pp. 9-10.

thought.[2] He claims that embezzlement is explained by a nonshareable financial problem, occupation of a position of trust, and access to cultural justifications for theft. What Cressey calls a "nonshareable financial problem," which may result from gambling or living beyond one's means, may be seen as a sign of moral weakness or pathology by others. Such a problem may well arise more commonly in the lives of individuals with certain personality traits or certain childhood experiences. Cressey's research was not designed to determine whether such differences existed between trust violators and others.

Cressey and Sutherland provide no supporting evidence for their assumption that psychological explanations of white collar crime are inadequate; however, others who have proposed that psychological variables do explain white collar crime also provide little empirical support for their position. For example, the Chamber of Commerce of the United States suggests that some cases of business crime might be explained by a "rotten apple theory"—the idea that in some people there is an inborn predisposition to defraud others whenever the opportunity arises.[3] No evidence to support this position is provided. Reckless, one sociologist who accepts the usefulness of some psychological theories of business crime, claims that such offenses can be explained in part by such personality elements as a willingness to violate the law or a low resistance to temptation.[4] Not only does he provide no supporting evidence for this position, but his argument appears to be tautological. If the only evidence for these supposed personality traits is that those who do violate the law are assumed to have such characteristics and those who do not violate the law are assumed not to, no independent evidence exists to show that these traits cause business crime. British criminologist Hermann Mannheim correctly states that there is little solid evidence to show psychological differences between white collar criminals and others and that one should not assume such differences in the absence of research

---

[2]Donald R. Cressey, *Other People's Money: A Study in the Social Psychology of Embezzlement* (Belmont: Calif.: Wadsworth Publishing Co., Inc., 1953, 1971), pp. 142-45.

[3]Chamber of Commerce of the United States, *A Handbook on White Collar Crime* (Washington, D.C.: Chamber of Commerce of the United States, 1974), p. 55.

[4]Walter C. Reckless, *The Crime Problem,* 5th ed. (New York: Appleton-Century-Crofts, 1973), p. 327.

on the issue.[5] The little work which has been done on the problem can now be examined.

Psychological Explanations of Business Crime

One attempt to explain business crime in psychological terms is that of psychiatrist Walter Bromberg.[6] He suggests that businessmen who violate the law have a feverish drive to make money and to vanquish their competitors. Their desire to climb to the top of the economic ladder is tied to a "fantasy of omnipotence," a sense of great power which outweighs their actual power. Bromberg explains white collar crime by "the myopia of business"; this phrase means that offending businessmen see the world through a limited perspective which is characterized by egocentricity, unconscious feelings of omnipotence, and little guilt. They are guided by the "common business ideal of success at any price."[7] He says that embezzlers have a neurotic drive to participate in the wealth of the corporation; he argues that their financial problem is only a rationalization for their theft and that the true cause of the financial problem and hence of the crime is their neurosis. This neurotic drive is partially attributed to a drive for wealth which results from a search for "unlimited parental love" which is rooted in childhood experiences.[8] Bromberg's arguments typify most psychiatric explanations of crime; they are *ad hoc* and inferential. A few criminals are examined and then guesses are made as to how they differ from unexamined noncriminals. Bromberg presents no data to show that in comparison to nonoffenders, those businessmen who violate the law have either a higher drive for profits or less guilt. His work is not designed to answer such questions.

Stuart Lottier presents one of the few psychological theories of business crime which relies on empirical data. He sees embezzlement as due in part to "tensions arising from biological and interpersonal as well as cultural conditions."[9] Lottier focuses on embezzlers who individually

[5]Hermann Mannheim, *Comparative Criminology* (Boston: Houghton Mifflin Company, 1965), p. 478-79.

[6]Walter Bromberg, *Crime and the Mind* (New York: Macmillan Publishing Co., Inc., 1965), pp. 377-89.

[7]*Ibid.*, p. 389.

[8]*Ibid.*, p. 258.

[9]Stuart Lottier, "Tension Theory and Criminal Behavior," *American Sociological Review*, 7 (December 1942), 840.

engage in apparently spontaneous acts of trust violation and to a lesser extent on those who engage in group embezzlement which is somewhat organized. His conclusions are drawn from his study of 50 embezzlers who faced charges in a Detroit court and were consequently subjected to medical and psychiatric examinations. The embezzlers had achieved higher educational levels and had higher IQs than the general population, were usually first offenders, had regular work records, were residentially stable, and apparently had good marriages. When apprehended, they were more often concerned with the trouble the arrest would cause their family than with harm to themselves. Although they could often give an explanation for their crimes, they usually realized that their explanations were inadequate.

Many businessmen work long hours and are ambitious, competitive, and aggressive. This combination produces strain, anxiety, and tension. Lottier argues that tension-producing conflicts in the organismic, psychic, interpersonal, and cultural conditions of the businessman's job cause embezzlement; he suggests that these four levels of tension are interrelated. Organismic hunger and sex drives create tension which either is internalized and leads to changes in physiological and psychic routines, or is externalized and leads to changes in behavioral routines. If it is internalized, medical or psychiatric problems may develop. If it is externalized, embezzlement may occur. Although Lottier argues that embezzlement is preceded by a state of increased tension, he makes it clear that this tension does not necessarily produce embezzlement; it may be discharged in other ways. Lottier wisely avoids the error of proposing that tension is a necessary and sufficient cause of embezzlement; Bromberg's theory implies that any businessman with an intense desire to achieve financial success will violate the law and that all who violate the law will have such a desire for success.

The common features of individual embezzlement which Lottier found in his research include: (1) repression of biologically determined desires which remain unsocialized; (2) the persistence of these desires as unconscious or conscious conflicts; (3) the occupation of a position of trust which provides an opportunity to embezzle in order to accommodate to the conflicts; (4) a situation which creates a painful increase in tension, leading the individual to seek relief; and (5) an absence of actual and perceived alternative ways to discharge or internalize the tension.[10] Lottier pays less attention to group embezzlement, which is organized to some extent. Because several individuals conspire to steal funds, there is no necessary increase in tension within any given individual prior to the crime. Such behavior is culturally conditioned, although tensions may exist at the organismic, psychic, or interpersonal levels as well.

Although Lottier's tension-reduction theory does not present a full explanation of embezzlement, it might well form part of a more complete theory of embezzlement or other business crimes. Lottier does not indicate why one individual will choose embezzlement as a means to reduce tension while another one internalizes tension. However, he does propose the significance of a potentially measurable variable; a study could be designed to test the tension level of a number of businessmen and then to determine whether those with the highest levels of tension actually violate the law most frequently.

One psychological factor which might be expected to be present among business offenders is guilt. However, guilt may be reduced where they have access to justifications for their behavior or where work group norms support theft under certain conditions. In his study of employee theft in a Midwestern electronics plant, Horning found that 80 of 88 workers admitted that they had stolen from the plant.[11] Of the 80 thieves, only 36 percent said that they felt guilty about the crime and 64 percent said that they felt no guilt. Only 16 percent of the 80 who had stolen said that *other* workers who stole from the plant were apt to feel guilty about their thefts. Workers were thus more likely to experience guilt themselves than to ascribe such feelings to others. Work group norms probably explain the absence of guilt in most of the employee thieves; their perceptions of those work group norms may also account for the finding that even fewer of them thought that other workers would feel guilty. The only other available evidence about guilt among business offenders comes from a study of incarcerated English white collar offenders which found that there was a relatively high degree of guilt among professional men and a relatively small amount of guilt among businessmen.[12] Whether this difference is due to the exclusion of professionals from their occupation after conviction, due to the greater

[11]Donald N. M. Horning, "Blue-Collar Theft: Conceptions of Property, Attitudes toward Pilfering, and Work Group Norms in a Modern Industrial Plant," in *Crimes against Bureaucracy*, ed. Erwin O. Smigel and H. Laurence Ross (New York: Van Nostrand Reinhold Company, 1970), pp. 60-61

[12]John C. Spencer, "White-Collar Crime," in *Criminology in Transition: Essays in Honor of Hermann Mannheim*, ed. T. Grygier, H. Jones, and John Spencer (London: Tavistock Publications, 1965), pp. 233-65.

availability of justifications for crime among the businessmen, or due to other factors cannot be determined.

In his study of OPA violations, Clinard states that differential association theory (which will be examined later in this chapter) explains much about white collar crime. However, he says that it fails to account for all such crime and particularly for individual differences in conformity within various business enterprises. He suggests that more attention should be paid to the personality traits of violators, since selective incorporation of cultural and business values is probably a function of personality. In other words, some but not all businessmen who learn values and norms favorable to violation of the law and who have the opportunity to violate the law will actually commit a crime.[13] Personality traits which may be important in determining participation in such crimes as black market activities include "egocentricity, emotional insecurity or feelings of personal inadequacy, negative attitudes toward other persons in general, the relative importance of status symbols of money as compared with nationalism, and the relative lack of importance of one's personal, family, or business reputation."[14]

Little evidence exists regarding the child-rearing practices to which business offenders were exposed when young. A study of 30 British white collar offenders found a noticeable absence of feelings of rejection or emotional deprivation among them.[15] Writing in 1916, Willem Bonger claimed that people who commit business crimes learn to be honest when young, but "they have learned also that the principal end in life is to grow rich, to succeed."[16] He saw a businessman's honesty not as moral honesty, but as honesty for the sake of personal advantage. He claimed that businessmen learned this pragmatic approach to honesty in the "bourgeois environment" created by the existing means of production. Bonger's position, developed well before others tried to explain crime in the business world, is provocative but untested. One might design a study to measure the social class background of businessmen as well as the content of their parents' teachings about honesty and success. Bonger's

[13]A similar position is taken in Richard Quinney, "The Study of White Collar Crime: Toward a Reorientation in Theory and Research," *Journal of Criminal Law, Criminology and Police Science,* 55 (June 1964), 213.

[14]Marshall B. Clinard, *The Black Market: A Study of White Collar Crime* (Montclair, N.J.: Patterson Smith, 1952, 1969), p. 310.

[15]Spencer, "White-Collar Crime," p. 261.

[16]Willem Bonger, *Criminality and Economic Conditions,* abridged with an introduction by Austin T. Turk (Bloomington: Indiana University Press, 1916, 1969), p. 136.

work would suggest that in comparison with law-abiding businessmen, those who violate the law would come from more bourgeois backgrounds, would have been exposed more to situational ethics rather than absolute moral pronouncements about honesty as children, and would have been more exposed to values emphasizing the importance of material success when they were young.

A recent study of alleged trust violators in the United States explored the frequency of "potentially troubling early experiences" such as death of a parent and poor home conditions and the frequency of "troubled behavior" such as learning difficulties and excitability. This study examined three executives who had allegedly been involved in industrial espionage and compared them with six men who acted as a control group. The trust violators had more problems than the controls, with most of their problems occurring during their childhoods.[17] Although this study is suggestive, the extremely small number of business offenders and nonoffenders examined makes it difficult to conclude with any certainty that the offenders actually differed from the nonoffenders in their childhood experiences.

Unsatisfactory as these few psychological studies of business crime are, they do show the potential value of introducing the psychological approach into the study of business crime. Few have tried to test such an approach with empirical data. In the following section, the theory of differential association will be discussed; this theory examines the psychological process of learning as it takes place in a social context.

Learning Business Crime

Some sociologists have suggested that business crime is caused by the learning of such cultural values as individualism, competitive achievement, exploitation, and monetary success.[18] One scholar claims that businessmen are led to "flirt with danger" because they desire a maximum profit with the least possible effort, they seek certainty, they want to be seen as "regular guys" by their competitors, they feel that if others can

---

[17]Richard H. Blum, *Deceivers and Deceived: Observations on Confidence Men and Their Victims, Informants and Their Quarry, Political and Industrial Spies and Ordinary Citizens* (Springfield, Ill.: C. C. Thomas, 1972), pp. 152-55.

[18]Donald R. Taft and Ralph W. England, Jr., *Criminology*, 4th ed. (New York: The Macmillan Company, 1964), pp. 205-6.

violate the law they should be able to also, and they think that the only sin is in being caught and that they can avoid that fate.[19]

Law-breaking in the American business world may be seen as normative. Group norms encourage such business crimes as employee theft and price-fixing. This is especially true if such norms exist in the absence of attachment to externally imposed norms about the legal means to achieve success. Without a code of business ethics which has teeth, there is no set of norms to counteract those norms which are conducive to business crime. After the convictions in the 1961 electrical equipment price-fixing case, neither the National Association of Manufacturers nor the Chamber of Commerce publicly condemned the violators.[20] One sociologist's comment 70 years ago that "criminaloids" moved "in an atmosphere of friendly approval" and that they could "still any smart of conscience with the balm of good fellowship and adulation" is still applicable today.[21]

Vilhelm Aubert suggests that a businessman faces contradictory expectations: a universalistic obligation as a citizen to obey the law, and a particularistic obligation as a businessman to avoid only the most blatant offenses and to resist the law whenever possible.[22] Aubert claims that the particularistic obligation to the firm generally guides the businessman's behavior. From his study of Oslo businessmen, he concludes that they generally hold a negative view of the law, although they admit that some of the laws regulating business are necessary. They condemn violation of the law in general, but they also justify violations in certain situations. Similarly, Sutherland found that during both world wars, American businessmen wanted to win the war but saw such particularistic considerations as profits and a stable market as more important than such universalistic considerations as patriotism and national security. As one corporation president said, "Patriotism is a very beautiful thing but it must not be permitted to interfere with business."[23]

[19]James R. Withrow, Jr. "Making Compliance Programs Work," *Business Lawyer*, 17 (July 1962), 880.

[20]Herbert A. Bloch and Gilbert Geis, *Man, Crime and Society*, 2nd ed. (New York: Random House, 1970), p. 312.

[21]Edward Alsworth Ross, *Sin and Society: An Analysis of Latter-Day Iniquity* (Boston: Houghton Mifflin, 1907), p. 57.

[22]Vilhelm Aubert, "White Collar Crime and Social Structure," *American Journal of Sociology*, 58 (November 1952), 268.

[23]Cited in Sutherland, *White Collar Crime*, p. 174.

C. Wright Mills refers to "structured immorality" as a cause of white collar crime. He feels that business crime results from a bad milieu in the impersonal corporate economy and that this leads to a lack of personal responsibility among businessmen.[24] White collar crime has also been described as being "functionally related to the operating principles of the organization or enterprise."[25] Norms and structures within the organization provide the conditions and justifications for criminal behavior. As a result, a businessman who is better assimilated into the business world is more apt to violate the law; a businessman who is new to the world of business is more likely to feel moral qualms about violating the law since he is less aware of colleague support for such behavior and is less attached to the values of business which are conducive to violation of the law. One study of attitudes toward bribery and payoffs by businessmen abroad found that the greatest amount of tolerance existed among experienced business executives enrolled in business school programs and the least tolerance existed among undergraduates who were enrolled in business programs and who were inexperienced in the ways of business.[26]

Business crime is often learned from superiors and from peers with whom one works. Learning in this social context is probably a more important determinant of business behavior than the personality of individual businessmen. The head of the Enforcement Division of the SEC has bluntly stated: "Our largest corporations have trained some of our brightest young people to be dishonest."[27] One study found that business executives thought that when an executive acted ethically, his behavior was due mostly to his own values and his ability to resist the temptation to violate the law; some credit was given to the influence of his superiors and to the effects of company policy. However, when an executive acted unethically, this was attributed to his superiors and to the climate of ethics in the industry. The behavior and attitudes of work peers were given some weight as a cause of unethical behavior but were not seen as very important determinants of ethical behavior.[28] The

[24]C. Wright Mills, *The Power Elite* (New York: Oxford University Press, 1957), p. 343.

[25]Richard D. Knudten, *Crime in a Complex Society: An Introduction to Criminology* (Homewood, Ill.: The Dorsey Press, 1970), p. 215.

[26]Michael C. Jensen, "Business Students Disagree on Bribes," *The New York Times,* March 27, 1976, p. 37.

[27]Cited in Louis M. Kohlmeier, "The Bribe Busters," *The New York Times Magazine,* September 26, 1976, p. 58.

[28]Raymond C. Baumhart, "How Ethical Are Businessmen?" *Harvard Business Review,* 39 (July-August 1961), 125-26.

types of social pressures which push some businessmen to violate the law are summarized as follows by one observer of the Equity Funding scandal:

> Corporations can and do create a moral tone that powerfully influences the thinking, conduct, values and even the personalities of the people who work for them. The tone is set by the men who run the company, and their corruption can quickly corrupt all else. A startling thing about Equity Funding is how rarely one finds, in a cast of characters big enough to make a war movie, a man who said, "No, I won't do that. It's wrong." As for the majority who were sucked in and drowned, their motives were many and mixed. The important thing is that the fraud unerringly pressed upon their weaknesses, some of which they were unaware of at the time, and quickly overthrew them almost before they realized what had happened.[29]

Executives convicted of price-fixing in the 1961 electrical industry case said that when they came to their jobs, they had found price-fixing to be an established practice. They claimed that they were pressured by the corporation to violate the law, although company presidents claimed after the convictions that the violators were self-aggrandizing men who had violated the moral precepts of the company in order to advance their own careers. The situation faced by the convicted violators is described well by Walter Goodman:

> The operative codes of behavior in business are never written down. They exist as what several of the electrical conspirators called "a way of life" in their industry, or as the "heritage" of executive-supplier relationships at Chrysler. The living code is an ever-shifting pattern of guidelines set by the necessities of the market, the conditions and traditions of the industry, the goals of the corporation, the aspirations of management and the nature of the executives themselves. These are complicated elements, blending economics and psychology with social attitudes; sometimes they are contradictory; often they run well beyond the businessman's control or understanding; and the result does not lend itself to display in 12-point type.[30]

Although they faced numerous pressures to violate the law, the convicted executives did say that their refusal to engage in price-fixing would probably have led to their transfer within the company rather than to

[29]William E. Blundell, "Equity Funding: 'I Did It for the Jollies,' " in *Swindled! Classic Business Frauds of the Seventies,* ed. Donald Moffitt (Princeton, N.J.: Dow Jones Books, 1976), p. 46.

[30]Walter Goodman, *All Honorable Men: Corruption and Compromise in American Life* (Boston: Little, Brown, 1963), p. 82.

their dismissal.[31] Had a number of executives asked for reassignment, it might have been possible to determine if they differed in psychological or social characteristics from those executives who acquiesced in the price-fixing conspiracy. However, if such executives did exist, no one has identified and studied them. Structural pressures to be a good company man and go along with the conspiracy may have been so strong that individual personality differences were unimportant. One executive convicted in the case later said, "I thought that we were more or less working on a survival basis in order to try to make enough to keep our plants and our employees."[32] The judge who sentenced the executives suggested that they had a sense of misplaced loyalty:

> . . . [T]hey were torn between conscience and an approved corporate policy, with the rewarding objectives of promotion, comfortable security and large salaries—in short, the organization or company man, the conformist, who goes along with his superiors and finds balm for his conscience in additional comforts and the security of his place in the corporate setup.[33]

One General Electric executive was even grateful that his company allowed him to stay on the job after his conviction, although he had his salary reduced from $74,000 to $27,600; this gratitude seems somewhat unusual, because the crime for which he was convicted provided him with no direct financial gain but did serve the interests of the company. The executives were such loyal company men that although "some of the men filed false travel claims, so as to mislead their superiors regarding the city they had visited [for meetings at which bids were rigged], they never asked for expense money to places more distant than those they had actually gone to—on the theory, apparently, that whatever else was occurring, it would not do to cheat the company."[34] Loyalty to a company is often regarded as a higher obligation than commitment to the law and is rewarded as such within the company. For instance, the employees of a company who falsified test data on airplane brakes were promoted; two workers who brought to official atten-

---

[31]Gilbert Geis, "White Collar Crime: The Heavy Electrical Equipment Antitrust Cases of 1961," in *Criminal Behavior Systems: A Typology*, ed. Marshall B. Clinard and Richard Quinney (New York: Holt, Rinehart and Winston, Inc., 1967), pp. 145-46.

[32]Cited in Geis, "White Collar Crime," p. 144.

[33]Cited in Fred J. Cook, *The Corrupted Land: The Social Morality of Modern America* (New York: Macmillan Publishing Co., Inc., 1966), p. 55.

[34]Geis, "White Collar Crime," p. 143.

tion the falsified data and the dangerousness of the brakes were forced to resign.[35]

Sutherland's theory of differential association is probably the most explicit form of a learning theory to be applied to business crime. He argues that white collar criminals learn their behavior by "direct or indirect association with those who already practice the behavior."[36] Businessmen learn a general ideology of profit and free enterprise, as well as specific techniques and justifications which are conducive to business crime. Along with this learning process, businessmen may be segregated from the law-abiding public prior to the commission of the offense; in this way, businessmen become immune to the criticism of others. Businessmen who read newspapers and journals hostile to government regulation of business are most apt to violate certain laws. Isolation from a pro-regulation point of view is more common in small towns that in large cities where there is a more diverse social life and a more cosmopolitan atmosphere. Executives in large cities are more accepting of government regulation than executives in small towns.[37] In one study of violations of the law by New England shoe manufacturers, the percentage of violators decreased as the size of the town in which a firm was located increased. For towns with a population under 5,000, 10 percent of the firms violated the law; for towns between 5,000 and 10,000, 8.5 percent violated the law; for towns between 10,000 and 25,000, 4.3 percent violated the law; for towns between 25,000 and 100,000, 2.3 percent violated the law; and for towns with a population in excess of 100,000, 2.6 percent violated the law.[38] These differences have been attributed to variations in the attitudes toward government regulation of business in the different settings.

Reckless and Dinitz attribute white collar crime to the insulation of businessmen from certain fundamental values which would normally be learned in the family or in reference groups.[39] Bonger has also argued that business offenders are immune to social disapproval because of

---

[35]Kermit Vandiver, " 'Why Should My Conscience Bother Me?' " in Robert L. Heilbroner and others, *In the Name of Profit: Profiles in Corporate Irresponsibility* (Garden City, N.Y.: Doubleday & Company, Inc., 1972), pp. 3-31.

[36]Edwin H. Sutherland, "White Collar Criminality," *American Sociological Review,* 5 (February 1940), 10.

[37]Robert E. Lane, *The Regulation of Businessmen: Social Conditions of Government Economic Control* (New Haven: Yale University Press, 1954), pp. 102-3.

[38]*Ibid.,* p. 103.

[39]Cited in Knudten, *Crime in a Complex Society,* p. 215.

their position in society.[40] An unresolved contradiction apparently exists here. Lane, Reckless and Dinitz, and Bonger all suggest that white collar crime arises from *insulation from certain values*, whereas scholars such as Sutherland and Taft and England suggest that white collar crime is caused by *learning certain values* such as monetary success and ambition.

Sutherland resolves this apparent contradiction in his theory of differential association. This theory explores the *ratio* of definitions favorable to violation of the law to definitions unfavorable to violation of the law. In other words, businessmen are exposed to a multitude of values and norms. Some values and norms support certain business crimes, and others condemn such crimes. In Sutherland's view, a business crime will occur when the ratio is weighted toward the definitions favorable to violation of the law, even though definitions unfavorable to violation of the law will also exist in the violator's mind. If the businessman *learns* definitions favorable to violation of the law, he may violate the law. However, he may also violate the law if he is *insulated* from definitions unfavorable to violation of the law. Either experience will change the ratio in a way to increase the likelihood of crime. Both types of definition must be considered in order to assess the chance that a given businessman will violate the law.

The value of differential association theory as an explanation of white collar crime has been examined by a number of sociologists. Clinard claims that most of the black market violations under the OPA controls were learned in association with others. Definitions of the situation and justifications for the crime were transmitted from one businessman to another through conversations and through descriptions in the general press and in trade newspapers. Clinard proposes as evidence for this learning process the planning of certain black market crimes, common attitudes toward enforcement personnel, the lack of condemnation of violators, and the absence of real support for government regulations. However, these conditions do not constitute proof that violations spread through the process of differential association. The nature of the OPA regulations, the structure of the market, the dominant business ideology, and the opportunities for violations may have caused businessmen who were in similar circumstances to react in similar ways. Violations may have been structured rather than learned.

[40]Bonger, *Criminality and Economic Conditions*, pp. 134–42.

Clinard also feels that differential association theory has a number of shortcomings as an explanation of OPA violations. He says that attitudes toward the law are only one element in the process of law violation. As we saw earlier, he suggests that personality traits and early socialization experiences may also be important determinants of white collar crime. Differential association theory also fails to examine how a businessman who violates the law adjusts to his other roles, such as community leader and father-husband. The theory does not allow for the independent innovation of complex techniques of business crime, although some businessmen apparently invent new techniques rather than learning them from others. The theory also fails to explain why some businessmen who are familiar with the means to commit a crime and who associate with people who violate the law do not commit business crimes themselves.[41]

Cressey's study of trust violators also leads him to assess the theory of differential association. He finds that embezzlers did not learn techniques and skills for embezzlement in association with others, since they used the same skills for their crimes as they had used in performing their jobs honestly. However, the trust violators had learned rationalizations for their crimes from others and from the general culture. Nevertheless, Cressey finds that in at least four of every five cases, the embezzler could not specify the source of the justification he had used for his crime. Cressey concludes that the general emphasis of differential association theory is correct, although the associations of the violators did not change just prior to their theft in a way which produced an excess of definitions favorable to violation of the law. Cressey feels that it is useful to retain the idea of learning justifications for crime but to drop the idea of contacts with criminal behavior patterns as an explanation of trust violation.

Relatively little empirical support now exists for the theory of differential association as an explanation for business crime. The theory suffers from an abstract quality which almost precludes testing it. Still, it does draw attention to the role of learning certain values and norms, as well as skills and techniques, in the genesis of business crime. This learning process is particularly important in providing businessmen with rationalizations and justifications for their violation of the law.

[41]Clinard, *The Black Market,* p. 309.

Justifying Business Crime

Although criminals may be guided by social norms which encourage antisocial behavior, some research on juvenile delinquents shows that they share many norms and values with law-abiding youths.[42] Delinquents are similar to youths who do not violate the law in their attachment to prescriptive norms ("thou shalt do this"), but differ in attachment to proscriptive norms ("thou shalt not do this"). In other words, delinquents and nondelinquents aspire to the same goals and share the same values, but they differ in their willingness to modify or "stretch" certain social norms in order to reach their goals. This difference in proscriptive norms is reflected in the "techniques of neutralization" or "vocabularies of adjustment" which are more common among delinquents than among nondelinquents.[43] Techniques of neutralization are justifications or rationalizations about the appropriateness of law-violating behavior under certain conditions. They are used to justify an act prior to its commission so that the offender does not have to make a direct assault on a dominant social norm.[44] The justification allows the offender to deny criminal intent and to maintain a noncriminal self-concept. "In order to violate the commandment, 'Thou shalt not steal,' the violator must have recourse to other commandments which deflect the original rule or provide exceptions. Even the most serious, premeditated crime seems to require some social legitimation before it can be carried out."[45] Evidence suggests that businessmen also employ such techniques of neutralizing the law to justify their crimes.

To the extent that a businessman has access to justifications for criminal behavior which other businessmen do not have access to, he will be more likely to violate the law. Techniques of neutralization may be even more important in explaining business crime than in explaining

[42]For example, see James F. Short, Jr., and Fred L. Strodtbeck, *Group Process and Gang Delinquency* (Chicago: University of Chicago Press, 1965); and Travis Hirschi, *Causes of Delinquency* (Berkeley: University of California Press, 1969).

[43]"Techniques of neutralization" is a term used in Gresham Sykes and David Matza, "Techniques of Neutralization: A Theory of Delinquency," *American Sociological Review*, 22 (December 1957), 664-70. "Vocabularies of adjustment" is a term used in Cressey, *Other People's Money.*

[44]Sykes and Matza, "Techniques."

[45]Erwin O. Smigel and H. Laurence Ross, "Introduction," in Smigel and Ross, *Crimes against Bureaucracy*, p. vi.

juvenile delinquency, because businessmen probably have a stronger need to deny criminal intent. Not only are their self-concepts more clearly noncriminal, but the general public probably regards them as noncriminal unless evidence to the contrary exists. On the other hand, juveniles are probably less apt to have strong noncriminal self-concepts because they lack experience in legitimate social roles; also, to an extent juveniles are expected to engage in a limited amount of antisocial behavior.

The first systematic use of the concept of justifications for crime was employed in a study of business crime, Donald R. Cressey's research on trust violators.[46] Rationalizations prior to the act of embezzlement were used by all the trust violators Cressey interviewed. These justifications were usually abandoned once the crime had been committed. Vocabularies of adjustment allowed previously noncriminal employees to engage in otherwise unacceptable behavior. Indeed, one element in Cressey's explanation of trust violation was that embezzlers "apply to their own conduct . . . verbalizations which enable them to adjust their conceptions of themselves as trusted persons with their conceptions of themselves as users of the entrusted funds or property."[47] Justifications for embezzlement were adaptations of general cultural definitions of when crime might be acceptable; these general definitions were then applied to specific situations.

One common method for justifying embezzlement is to claim that the money is being "borrowed"; the common business practice of temporarily using funds which clearly do not belong to a businessman is pointed to as a justification for such "borrowing." This rationalization distinguishes the embezzler's use of funds from stealing, since there is no criminal intent to deprive the owner of the money permanently, but only to use the money until it can be returned. However, auditors generally feel that it is more difficult to return stolen funds undetected than to take them in the first place. Another rationalization an embezzler may use is to tell himself that he faces a specific and unusual emergency and that he differs from "other embezzlers" who waste money on "broads, booze and bets." Not only does he thus draw on the cultural stereotype of embezzlers so as to differentiate himself from them, but he also justifies his behavior by the socially acceptable requirement to support his family in time of need. A third rationalization is that there is much unethical

[46]Cressey, *Other People's Money.*
[47]*Ibid.,* p. 30.

behavior in the business world and that his behavior is no worse than that of many other businessmen. This justification for law-violating behavior as part of a general and widespread immorality is fairly common in the business world. Corporate executives often justify foreign bribery by claiming that all firms operating abroad engage in similar practices. The executive director of the New York State Association of Service Stations responded in a similar way to a study which showed that more than half of a group of repair shops had cheated their customers; he said that "only a small percentage of repairmen are fraudulent operators. Sure you'll find some dishonesty, but you'll find some dishonesty among doctors, lawyers or any type of people."[48] Such vocabularies of adjustment allow businessmen to maintain a noncriminal self-concept, even in the face of clear evidence to the contrary. Long after they have "borrowed" more money than they could ever realistically repay, embezzlers remain hopeful of doing so. Eventually they may get in "too deep" and have to adjust their self-concept and see themselves as criminals.

One justification for some business crimes is that no injury is done by the act. A study of employee thieves in a Midwestern electronics plant found that work group norms supported theft by defining property in the plant in a particular way. The plant contained property which was readily pilferable and which could be used by workers in nonwork situations. The workers conceived of plant property in three broad categories —company property, personal property, and property of uncertain ownership. Some property clearly belonged to the company or to specific employees. Other property, such as unmarked clothing or money, could not be identified as belonging to the company or to any particular worker and was therefore of uncertain ownership. Some company-owned property which was small, inexpensive, expendable, and plentiful was seen as belonging to no one in particular. Definition of property was affected by the degree to which the company regulated the flow of material; there was less uncertainty about ownership when regulation was tight. Although there were three broad categories of property, there could only be two victims of a theft, the company or a worker. Workers held a strong norm against theft from individuals; 80 percent of the workers felt that theft from a worker was more serious than theft from the company, and the rest felt that the two types of theft were equally

[48]Frances Cerra, "11 of 24 Auto-Repair Shops Pass a Test on Honesty," *The New York Times*, December 8, 1975, pp. 1, 50.

serious. When property was of uncertain ownership, the thief did not have to deny any victim and could argue that no harm was being done by taking the property. Group norms tolerated the theft of "valueless" property of uncertain ownership, although norms also limited theft to what was needed for personal use and to what would not attract the attention of supervisors. Work group norms also helped workers to deny a victim and to deny injury, thus reducing the constraints of the competing legal norm against theft.[49]

Studies of theft by hotel workers and by dock workers led to similar conclusions about the use of rationalizations prior to the commission of theft. Hotel workers frowned upon theft of personal property belonging to guests, but they felt that the theft of hotel property was acceptable.[50] A study of theft by dock workers revealed that work group norms held some cargo to be inviolable, e.g., personal baggage, but other property to be an acceptable target for theft, e.g., boxes addressed to large firms and packages covered by insurance.[51] Goods which were defined as pilferable were seen as "a morally justified addition to wages" or "an entitlement due from exploiting employers."[52] There was an informal norm limiting theft to an amount no greater than the worker's legitimate wages. This limit gave workers a goal to aspire to, but it protected the work group from disciplinary action by limiting the amount of property stolen from the dock. Managers accepted a certain amount of theft but took action if the amount was exceeded.

Business crimes may be facilitated by available rationalizations that either deny injury from the crime or deny the victim of the crime by claiming that he deserved to suffer. Embezzlers and employee thieves often rationalize their thefts by claiming that their company deserves to have its property stolen because of its exploitation of workers and customers; the impersonality of the large corporation may reinforce such a rationalization. Employees may also justify theft by saying that they plan to return the money or that the stolen property would have been discarded anyway. A claim of unfair rewards for job performance may

[49]Horning, "Blue-Collar Theft," pp. 55-62.

[50]Gerald Mars, "Hotel Pilferage: A Case Study in Occupational Theft," in *Sociology of the Workplace: An Interdisciplinary Approach,* ed. Malcolm Warner (London: Allen & Unwin, 1973), pp. 200-10.

[51]Gerald Mars, "Dock Pilferage: A Case Study in Occupational Theft," in *Deviance and Social Control,* ed. Paul Rock and Mary McIntosh (London: Tavistock Publications, 1974), pp. 209-28.

[52]*Ibid.,* p. 224.

also help offenders justify their thefts and avoid self-definition as a criminal; studies of embezzlers have concluded that feelings of being underpaid, unappreciated, overworked, and badly treated often preceded the theft of funds.[53]

A study of lawyers in New York City suggests that they may exploit low-status clients if they define them as expendable, one-shot clients who are unlikely to be sources of future income.[54] This finding might tentatively be extended to contexts in which businessmen deal with clients who are of low social status and with whom there is little chance of future business transactions. Under such circumstances, businessmen may exploit customers. This might be true of used car dealers or door-to-door salesmen. Exploitation may also be more common if the customer is seen as ignorant. This is especially likely to be the case when repairs are too complex for common understanding, as with car or watch repairs. A 1941 study of radio repairs found that women were more likely than men to be cheated by repair shops because they were thought to be more ignorant of the functioning of radios.[55] A similar finding emerged from a study of watch repair shops. To reinforce a customer's feeling of ignorance, watch repairmen and car mechanics may use sophisticated-looking equipment and technical explanations of malfunctions to confuse the customer. One proprietor of a radio repair school told an author of the study, "It will take a year to learn the radio business, but we can teach you enough so you can fool the public in about three months."[56] Another instructor in the school reinforced this, saying, "Nine-tenths of the stuff that goes into a radio when it is serviced is something the radio didn't need."[57]

In another study of businessmen's attitudes toward customers, 442 ghetto retail merchants were asked whom they blame for various merchant-customer problems such as credit and pricing.[58] If the merchants had blamed customers for bad relations, they might have been able to

[53]Cressey, *Other People's Money,* pp. 57–66; and "Postwar Embezzler Is Younger, Lives Faster, Is Less Inclined to Suicide," *Journal of Accountancy,* 90 (October 1950), 344.

[54]Jerome Carlin, *Lawyers' Ethics* (New York: Russell Sage Foundation, 1966), pp. 66–73.

[55]Roger William Riis and John Patric, *Repairmen Will Get You If You Don't Watch Out* (New York: Doubleday, Doran and Co., Inc., 1942).

[56]Cited in Riis and Patric, *Repairmen,* p. 154.

[57]Cited in Riis and Patric, *Repairmen,* pp. 154–55.

[58]Peter H. Rossi and others, "Between White and Black: The Faces of American Institutions in the Ghetto," in *Supplemental Studies for the National Advisory Commission on Civil Disorders* (Washington, D.C.: U.S. Government Printing Office, 1968), pp. 69–215.

"deny the victim" and exploit their customers more easily. However, few merchants did blame their customers for such problems. Although the merchants did not have access to such justifications for exploitation of customers, it is possible that further study would reveal that those merchants who did blame customers for bad relations were most apt to exploit them. This study also found that of all the occupational groups interviewed—retail merchants, major employers, school teachers, welfare workers, grassroots politicians, and the police—the merchants were the most apt to describe blacks as "violent, criminal, and unreasonable in their desires for equality."[59] Also, 61 percent of the merchants felt that blacks had to be watched more closely while in the store than whites because they were more apt to steal; only 35 percent disagreed with this. Eighty percent of the merchants thought that shops in black communities had to be especially burglary-proof, whereas only 17 percent disagreed. There was a slight tendency to agree that blacks were more likely than whites to cash bad checks. Thus many merchants felt that race was a relevant consideration in merchant-customer relations. This might suggest that to the extent that merchants do exploit customers, they might exploit black customers more often than white ones because they can more easily deny them as victims. Such discrimination might take the form of short-weighting, excessive credit charges, or the sale of adulterated food.

Another type of justification for violation of the law is to deny the legitimacy of the law which regulates behavior. This may be done by making distinctions between what is legal and what is moral. One executive involved in the electrical equipment price-fixing conspiracy said, "One of the problems of business is what is normal practice, not what is the law. If it's normal practice, it's ethical—not legal, but ethical."[60] Another executive involved in the conspiracy stated:

> "One faces a decision, I guess, at such times, about how far to go with company instructions, and since the spirit of such meetings only appeared to be correcting a horrible price level situation, that there was not an attempt to damage customers, charge excessive prices, there was no personal gain in it for me, the company did not seem actually to be defrauding . . . *morally,* it did not seem quite as bad as might be inferred by the definition of the activity itself."[61]

[59]*Ibid.,* p. 129.
[60]Cited in Cook, *The Corrupted Land,* p. 39.
[61]Cited in Goodman, *All Honorable Men,* p. 33. Emphasis added here.

An attorney for one of the convicted executives tried to convince the judge that the government's demand for a jail sentence for his client was "cold-blooded" because it would place a respectable man in prison with "common criminals who have been convicted of embezzlement and other serious crimes."[62] A "real crime" was evidently one committed against the company by an employee, not one committed by the company against customers and competitors.

Business offenders may maintain a noncriminal definition of their behavior and themselves because the law is rarely enforced and then only in flagrant cases. Businessmen may ask, "If my behavior were really criminal, wouldn't the law punish me?" The attitude that crime is only that behavior which is actually punished and a criminal only a person who is convicted is common in the world of business. Still, those involved in the electrical price-fixing conspiracy were clearly aware that they were violating the law. This is evident from their use of code names in meetings with co-conspirators. They also called co-conspirators only from public telephones in order to avoid wiretaps, met in places distant from their companies' home offices, sent mail to co-conspirators in plain envelopes rather than in business envelopes, and falsified expense accounts to conceal where meetings had taken place. Just as one study of shoplifters showed that they refused to see themselves as criminals until store managers and police officers forced them to abandon their illusions that their behavior was "merely 'naughty' or 'bad,' " corporate executives may also maintain a noncriminal self-concept until law enforcement officials force a change in that view.[63]

However, the enforcement of the law often engenders hostility among businessmen. Antitrust laws are seen as inconsistent, hypocritical, poorly defined, and rarely enforced. Although the interpretation of these laws is constantly evolving, many businessmen who violate the law are aware that they are taking a risk when they engage in certain actions. They test the limits of the law and try to keep "just inside an imaginary boundary thought to separate the condoned from the condemned."[64] Price-fixing is a clear violation of the law which is regularly prosecuted by the Department of Justice's Antitrust Division, but even businessmen who are charged with this crime often claim that the law is excessively vague.

[62]Cited in Geis, "White Collar Crime," p. 140.

[63]Mary Owen Cameron, *The Booster and the Snitch* (New York: The Free Press, 1955), p. 161.

[64]"Antitrust Criminal Sanctions," *Columbia Journal of Law and Social Problems,* 3 (1967), 156.

Compliance or noncompliance with the law by a businessman is partly determined by his attitudes toward the law and toward law enforcers. This may take the form of "condemnation of the condemners."[65] Those who are responsible for enforcement of the law are condemned as hypocritical or spitefully motivated. Businessmen express contempt for the law, for government, or for law enforcement agents. They often see the government as impeding their activities and sometimes express open bitterness about the "bureaucratic snoopers" who regulate their behavior.[66] Such attitudes may well reduce the effectiveness of legal constraints on the behavior of businessmen.

Robert Lane has speculated on some of the reasons why businessmen may violate the law. He suggests that the ambiguity of the law may create situations in which strongly held norms are in conflict with vaguely defined laws, leading some businessmen to "probe the law's farthest limits."[67] Such violations might not necessarily be deliberate if the law is new, evolving, or unclear. Furthermore, the law might be so complex that honest ignorance exists among businessmen. Although they might find it difficult to follow new developments in the law, they might also use the changing nature of the law as an excuse for remaining ignorant of even those laws which are clearly defined and consistently enforced. Lane concluded that ignorance of the law was not a primary reason for violations. He also considered that violations might result from the expense of complying with regulations; the cost of record-keeping might make it more costly to abide by the law than to risk the consequences of punishment for violation of the law. However, his interviews with 25 executives of shoe manufacturing firms showed that few of them thought that the expense of complying with the law was a significant cause of violation of government regulations.

Lane explored the possibility that businessmen might justify their violations by claiming that regulation of business was not a legitimate function of government. In his content analysis of a business journal (the 1934-40 and 1946-48 issues of *Connecticut Industry*), he found a commonly expressed feeling that government regulation was coercive, arbitrary, and incompatible with such basic American values as "fair profit" and "free enterprise." By referring to such values as "American," the businessman appeals to a higher loyalty. Lane's analysis of the

[65]Sykes and Matza, "Techniques," p. 668.

[66]Morton Mintz and Jerry S. Cohen, *America, Inc.: Who Owns and Operates the United States* (New York: The Dial Press, 1971), p. 266.

[67]Lane, *Regulation of Businessmen*, p. 95.

business journal showed that 77 percent of the references to regulatory measures were unfavorable, 14 percent were neutral, and 9 percent were favorable. Of those few positive references, 56 percent claimed that regulation was necessary and in the public interest, 40.2 percent claimed that regulation was good for business, and 3.8 percent claimed that the regulation process was efficient. The bulk of the 1,344 references were unfavorable; they criticized the regulations for being confused or unsuccessful in achieving their purpose (18.2 percent), coercive (18.0 percent), detrimental to business recovery or prosperity (16.5 percent), politically motivated or biased (9.8 percent), expensive to manufacturers (9.5 percent), administered by ineffective personnel (8.7 percent), too extensive (8.7 percent), poorly administered, with excessive red tape (6.8 percent), and a source of uncertainty (4.0 percent). Overall, 50 percent of the negative references referred to ways in which regulations were detrimental to manufacturers, 34.7 percent referred to ways in which they harmed the public good, and 15.5 percent referred to the poor administration of the regulations. Lane found a decline in unfavorable comments on the regulations over time, from a high of 88 percent unfavorable comments in 1935 to a low of 48 percent in 1948.[68] Evidently the business point of view reflected in the journal changed over the years, possibly because of better administration of the regulations and possibly because businessmen grew accustomed to such government regulation.

If businessmen feel "ideologically deprived" by government regulation because they think that the law is unfair and unduly restrictive of the economic forces to which they have a strong commitment, they may violate the law.[69] Businessmen often wrap themselves in the cloak of open competition and free enterprise, even when they violate the law in an effort to destroy their competitors.[70] They may justify such unfair labor practices as interference with union organization or failure to bargain in good faith by citing the sacred nature of free enterprise and private ownership of property; business ideology supports the notion that the firm belongs to the owner and that he should be able to run it as he wishes, with discontented workers leaving their jobs for other positions if they wish.[71] One piece of convoluted logic in which free enterprise was used to justify criminal behavior is the following statement

[68]*Ibid.*, pp. 38–40.
[69]*Ibid.*, pp. 21–24.
[70]Sutherland, *White Collar Crime*, pp. 61, 70, 75, 84.
[71]*Ibid.*, p. 145.

by one of the convicted electrical company executives: "No one attending the gathering [of the conspirators] was so stupid he didn't know the meetings were in violation of the law. But it is the only way a business can be run. It is free enterprise."[72] How a conspiracy to stabilize prices and increase profits by eliminating competition can be called free enterprise is a puzzle.

Although some businessmen oppose government regulation as a violation of the free enterprise system, regulatory agencies often serve the interests of the industries they supposedly regulate. As a result, businessmen often oppose any attempt to restore free enterprise by "deregulation." In 1975 President Gerald R. Ford called for less federal regulation of the airlines, claiming that the Civil Aeronautics Board "now serves to stifle competition, increase cost to travelers, makes the industry less efficient than it could be and denies large segments of the American public access to lower cost air transportation."[73] Instead of welcoming the opportunity for the return of free enterprise to the air industry, a spokesman for the Air Transport Association stated that such a change would "adversely affect millions of passengers and shippers, thousands of businesses in hundreds of communities, the reliable transportation of the mail, the welfare of 300,000 airline employees, millions of shareholders, investors holding billions of dollars of airline debt, aircraft manufacturers and suppliers and will endanger the financial integrity of the nation's vital airport system."[74] According to this representative of the airline industry, the country could not afford free enterprise in the industry. Something other than the public interest may have prompted this statement, since the spokesman added that the airlines were also worried about a drop in profits if deregulation became a reality.

Compliance with the law by businessmen is in part a function of how fair they perceive the law to be. There is some evidence that laws which are seen as unfair will be violated with greater frequency than laws which are thought to be fair. A 1944 survey in ten cities tested the attitudes of 179 gasoline dealers toward OPA regulations on gasoline rationing. Only 45 percent of the dealers thought that rationing was necessary. The rest thought that the regulations were unfair for various reasons. Clinard believed that these reasons were "rationalizations for the viola-

---

[72]Cited in Cook, *The Corrupted Land*, p. 37.

[73]"Ford Proposes Cut in Controls over Airline Service and Fares," *The New York Times*, October 9, 1975, p. 37.

[74]*Ibid.*

tions which were occurring."[75] Most commonly mentioned was the idea that there was no need for rationing because there was enough gasoline for everyone. The second most commonly mentioned reason was that the mere existence of a black market in gasoline showed that there was a plentiful supply. Although there was no evidence on actual rationing violations, the 179 dealers were asked how much gasoline they thought was being sold on the black market. Those who thought that the regulations were unnecessary estimated that more gasoline was being sold in violation of the law than did those who thought the regulations were necessary. This may indicate that perceived unfairness of the law is related to actual violations, if one assumes that a dealer's estimate of how much gasoline was being sold illegally reflected his own involvement in the black market. More generally, Clinard found evidence of extensive OPA violations by businessmen, attributing these in part to business-men's feelings that the law had to be violated in order to make a fair profit during wartime conditions, although data showed that there were generally higher profit levels during the war at all levels of production and distribution.

Some businessmen who violated OPA regulations did so by interpreting the rules in a selective and distorted manner. They were able to main-tain a noncriminal self-concept by saying that although the *formal rule* might establish a particular control, the *intent* of the government was not to control the good or service. This distinguishing between formal regulation and actual intent was encouraged by confusing regulations and by changes in rules over time. Violations were also justified by state-ments that money would be lost through compliance, that no one in the industry obeyed the rules, and that certain regulations were illogical. Some businessmen claimed that compliance took too much time or disturbed the production process, that regulation was a form of govern-ment dictatorship over business, that particular regulations were unfair, that high profit levels had to be maintained at all costs, or that the firm's reputation was relatively unimportant.[76] Many of the justifications for violation of OPA regulations were thus related to perceived unfair-ness of the law.

Additional light is cast on the way in which perceived fairness of the law affects violation of the law by a questionnaire study of landlords in

[75]Clinard, *The Black Market*, p. 169.

[76]George Katona, *Price Control and Business* (Bloomington, Ind.: The Principia Press, Inc., 1945).

Honolulu. The law regarding rent control in that city established three categories of control: (1) a fair-rent date ceiling, which took into account inflation only with regard to substantial increases in direct operating costs (the most rigid of the regulations from the landlords' perspective); (2) a fair-return ceiling, which took into account post-World War II inflation to some extent (a less rigid regulation); and (3) a new-construction ceiling, which took into account much of the post-war inflation (the least rigid type of regulation). When landlords were classified by type of rent-control regulation to which they were subject, there was great variation in the proportion who viewed their own situation as unfair: 70 percent of the fair-rent date landlords, 54 percent of the fair-return landlords, and 40 percent of the new-construction landlords. Thus, higher proportions of landlords in the more rigidly controlled situations felt unfairly treated by the law. Violations of the rent-control regulations were also more common among landlords in the more rigidly controlled situations: 29 percent with a fair-rent date ceiling reported violations of the law, in contrast to 15 percent with a fair-return ceiling and only 7 percent with a new-construction ceiling. Thus those in the more rigidly controlled situations were both more apt to feel they were treated unfairly and also more apt to violate the law. None of the 232 landlords who reported violations of the law thought that the regulation to which he was subject was fair, but 34 percent of the 818 nonviolators felt that the ceiling to which he was subject was fair. Violations were not related to the landlord's view about rent control as a general policy. However, the fact that the law treated landlords in different ways made it seem unfair, and this perceived unfairness was used to justify violation of the law.[77]

One form of behavior which is sometimes a business crime is tax evasion. A survey of 1,698 Americans in the 1940s found that 57 percent of the men and 40 percent of the women admitted to some form of tax evasion. Within this nonrandom group, which was weighted toward middle- and upper-income individuals, businessmen and lawyers were the occupational categories most apt to admit tax evasion.[78] In the mid-1960s, two-thirds of the Americans prosecuted for criminal tax fraud were self-employed; most were in the medical, legal, and accounting

[77]Harry V. Ball, "Social Structure and Rent Control Violations," *American Journal of Sociology*, 65 (May 1960), 598-604.

[78]James S. Wallerstein and Clement J. Wyle, "Our Law-Abiding Law-Breakers," *National Probation*, 25 (March-April 1947), 107-12.

professions.[79] Although there are no empirical studies of businessmen's attitudes toward the payment of taxes, there is "a firmly established American custom of tax evasion" which is a result of culturally available justifications:

> . . . [W]e must pay tribute to American inventiveness in concocting balms and unguents for abrasions of the taxpayer's conscience. The variety is admirable; there is a specific salve for every type of citizen. For example, if your political party happens to be in office, you recount to yourself the manifold services you are rendering to it and through it to the nation; why not leave taxes to the others? If your party is out of office, you ask why you should exacerbate the follies of the administration by providing funds for imbeciles to squander. If you are conservative, you oppose change by keeping your money where it is. If a progressive, you remind yourself that tomorrow new demands will inevitably be made on your purse. If opulent, you have proved you know how to use your money better than any politician can use it for you. If poor, you need it more than the government does. If married, you must take care of your family; if single, you have no one else to take care of you. And so the theme flows on and on through inexhaustible variations.[80]

Businessmen may also justify tax evasion by the idea of free enterprise, which includes the right of individuals not to have private property confiscated by the government. Businessmen may cheat on their tax returns through the padding of expense accounts, justifying this by saying that the tax structure is confiscatory and that "it's the executive who knows how much he should spend to do business."[81] Another justification for tax evasion is that the victim—the government, although it is more accurately the people—is large and impersonal; the claim may be made that no individual human being is being harmed. Data show that attitudes toward theft from large and impersonal organizations, especially the government, are more tolerant than attitudes toward theft from small and more personalized organizations.[82] This justification may be

---

[79]The President's Commission on Law Enforcement and Administration of Justice, *Task Force Report: Crime and Its Impact—An Assessment* (Washington, D.C.: U.S. Government Printing Office, 1967), p. 113.

[80]Edmond Cahn, *The Moral Decision: Right and Wrong in Light of American Law* (Bloomington: Indiana University Press, 1956), p. 168.

[81]An unidentified businessman cited in "Expense Accounts," *Harvard Business Review*, 38 (March-April 1960), 170.

[82]Erwin O. Smigel, "Public Attitudes toward Stealing as Related to the Size of the Victim Organization," *American Sociological Review*, 21 (June 1956), 320-27.

buttressed by the argument that the government is not truly representative of the people and that taxpayers do not really control how their tax dollars are spent. Thus attitudes toward both the government as victim and toward the law itself may encourage businessmen as well as private citizens to evade taxes. Although supporting data are lacking, businessmen may cheat more on taxes than other citizens because they have greater access to techniques for neutralizing the law. Swiss bankers, who sometimes handle the fruits of tax evasion, are also well-equipped with justifications for their actions, as can be seen from the following selection from Paul Erdman's novel, *The Billion Dollar Sure Thing:*

> The motives of all of these people were essentially the same. They sought protection from immoral intrusions into their private affairs. What could be more private than money? Nothing, said the Swiss, absolutely nothing. And they really meant it, with evangelical fervour. Sure, perhaps some of this money which sought refuge from prying eyes was untaxed. Perhaps it had been illegally smuggled out of Latin America or Asia into Switzerland. Maybe it was stolen. This was not Switzerland's concern. If nations insisted upon introducing unreasonably high taxes or foreign exchange controls limiting one of man's God-given freedoms to do what he likes with the money he amasses, that was not their fault. Also a crime in Chicago was not necessarily one in Zurich. History had always proved that in money matters the Swiss were right and the rest of the world had been consistently wrong. Little did the world realize the benefits it accrued from this attitude. For it was banks like the General Bank of Switzerland which took what the incurable cynics insisted upon calling "black money," bleached it, and put it to work productively; money which otherwise would have remained hidden and idle. Thus Switzerland was able to mobilize capital, lend it to industry, and raise the living standards of the world.[83]

Businessmen thus neutralize the constraints of the law and maintain a noncriminal self-concept in a variety of ways. One means for doing this is to claim that their behavior, even when it violates the law, is not really criminal because it is not treated as criminal by the legal system. The following chapter will look at the treatment of business crime by the legal system and explore the reasons why business crime is dealt with as it is.

---

[83]Paul E. Erdman, *The Billion Dollar Sure Thing* (New York: Pocket Books, 1973), pp. 143-44.

five

Business Crime
and the
Criminal Justice System

Business offenses rarely elicit harsh sanctions from the criminal justice system, although violations are defined as crimes and may be punished in the same way as traditional crimes. This chapter will examine the sparse data which exist on the reaction of the criminal justice system to crime in the business world and then examine some of the reasons for the differential treatment of businessmen and corporations.

Prosecution and Sentencing of Business Offenders

A few years ago corporate executives who bribed public officials in order to ease the construction of a New Jersey pipeline were convicted in a criminal court. They were punished with suspended sentences and five years of unsupervised probation; their corporation was fined.[1] This is a typical outcome of the occasional business offense which leads to a criminal conviction: lenient sentences for the offending individuals and a weak fine for the corporation. In recent cases involving companies found guilty of making illegal political contributions, fines have averaged about $4,000, a sum equivalent to about twelve seconds of gross income

---

[1]Morton Mintz, "A Colonial Heritage," in Robert L. Heilbroner and others, *In the Name of Profit: Profiles in Corporate Irresponsibility* (Garden City, N.Y.: Doubleday & Company, Inc., 1972), pp. 60-105.

for the companies which were fined.[2] Such punishments are not only lenient in absolute terms, but they are also lenient in comparison to sentences meted out to such common criminals as shoplifters and burglars. A chief teller in a New York City bank recently received a short prison term, of which he served twenty months, for his theft of $1.5 million from his bank. The justification for this light penalty was that he had cooperated with the authorities by showing them how to prevent a recurrence of the crime, that he had a stable family life, and that he would seek help for his compulsive gambling which had led to his theft.[3] Common thieves who steal much smaller sums of money often receive considerably longer prison sentences.

Data on the sentencing of white collar offenders in federal courts during 1971 show a pattern of lighter penalties for business crimes than for other types of offenses.[4] Defendants convicted of the following crimes received the following penalties:

Offense	Percent with jail sentence	Mean number of months
Auto theft	71%	36
Transporting stolen property	64%	48
Stealing from the mails	50%	31
Income tax evasion	35%	9.5
Embezzlement	22%	20
Securities fraud	16%	under 12

The conventional crimes of auto theft, transporting stolen property, and stealing from the mails led to jail sentences at least half of the time; sentences averaged about three years for these crimes. The three white collar crimes, including the business crimes of embezzlement and securities fraud, produced jail sentences much less frequently, and sentences were often less than one year. Many cases of income tax evasion uncovered by the IRS involve businessmen, especially accountants. The

[2]Charles H. McCaghy, *Deviant Behavior: Crime, Conflict, and Interest Groups* (New York: Macmillan Publishing Co., Inc., 1976), p. 220.

[3]"An Embezzler Tells of Treading a Twisted Trail," *The New York Times*, September 10, 1975, p. 72.

[4]Whitney North Seymour, Jr., *Why Justice Fails* (New York: William Morrow & Company, Inc., 1973), pp. 45–46.

selective prosecution of such cases produces a high conviction rate, although fewer than half of those who are convicted receive jail sentences and most of the sentences are less than one year. For example, 97 percent of those who were prosecuted for income tax evasion in 1966 were convicted. However, only 593 offenders were convicted in that year; 40 percent of them received jail sentences, but nearly all of those sentences were less than one year.[5]

Another study of the sentencing of white collar offenders looked at 645 cases in the Southern District of New York during a six-month period in 1972. This study also showed that white collar offenders received more lenient treatment than those who had committed conventional offenses.[6] Whereas 36 percent of the convicted white collar offenders received prison sentences, 53 percent of those convicted of nonviolent crimes and 80 percent of those convicted of violent crimes received prison sentences. The following table shows the sentences meted out in the Southern District of New York and in all federal courts in the nation during that six-month period:

Offense	Percent with jail sentence		Mean number of months	
	SDNY	Federal	SDNY	Federal
Bank embezzlement	23.2%	19.5%	18.0	21.3
IRS violation	35.4%	36.5%	5.9	10.4
Postal embezzlement	43.7%	19.0%	5.0	11.6
Securities fraud	66.7%*	21.5%	20.5	—
Securities theft	100.0%**	57.4%	36.5	38.7

*Percentage based on only nine cases
**Percentage based on only eight cases

These data indicate some variation in sentencing practices for different types of business crime. For the offenses for which there are a sufficient number of cases to examine, fewer than half of the convicted offenders received jail sentences; the sentences were generally under two years.

[5]The President's Commission on Law Enforcement and Administration of Justice, *Task Force Report: Crime and Its Impact—An Assessment* (Washington, D.C.: U.S. Government Printing Office, 1967), p. 114.

[6]Whitney North Seymour, Jr., "Social and Ethical Considerations in Assessing White-Collar Crime," *The American Criminal Law Review*, 11 (Summer 1973), 833-34.

When business offenders are convicted in criminal court, the most common sanction is either a suspended sentence with probation or a fine. Fines are often trivial in amount for corporations. In fact, usually the corporation has gained more financially from its crime than it pays in a fine if convicted. Small fines may be interpreted by corporate directors and executives as an indication that the offense is not regarded seriously by society or by the criminal justice system, since the firm retains the fruits of the crime and may even deduct the fine as a loss on tax returns. Treble damage suits in civil cases are usually a greater threat to the financial well-being of a corporation than are criminal fines. Fines are ineffective because they can be passed on to consumers in higher prices, although this might adversely affect the competitive position of the company in the marketplace. There may also be a loss of corporate goodwill as a result of a fine, although public awareness of corporate wrongdoing is probably minimal and is kept that way by the influence of businessmen on the mass media.

Fines levied against businessmen may be more financially burdensome than fines levied against corporations. However, many corporations provide free legal counsel for employees charged with crimes committed on behalf of the company. Also, some states permit corporations to indemnify or repay executives for fines which result from criminal cases, if the offender is not guilty of negligence or misconduct. The cost of indemnification is similar to an indirect fine against the company itself, and it can be passed on to consumers in higher prices or deducted from dividends paid to stockholders.

One federal law which sometimes leads to criminal prosecution is the Sherman Antitrust Act of 1890. This law gave concurrent jurisdiction in handling antitrust and restraint of trade cases to the Federal Trade Commission and the Antitrust Division of the Department of Justice. Only the Antitrust Division can prosecute criminal cases, but the FTC can recommend cases to it for action. However, in recent years the FTC has become more conservative in taking action. This is due to many factors, including inadequate resources for the investigation and development of cases, a high degree of bureaucratization, and the lack of a real sense of mission. During the 1960s, the average case took over four years from initial investigation until a cease-and-desist order was issued and appeals were made; some cases took as long as twenty years to complete, by which time the offensive behavior was no longer occurring.[7]

[7]Philip G. Schrag, *Counsel for the Deceived: Case Studies in Consumer Fraud* (New York: Pantheon Books, 1972), pp. 7–8.

Not only has the FTC failed to recommend the prosecution of many cases, but the Antitrust Division is also highly selective in its prosecution of cases, acting only against "willful violators." Willfulness is presumed if the rules of law are clear and established (e.g., the accused acted in obvious disregard of the law while aware that his actions were criminal). Prosecution may also be justified if there is serious harm to competitors or the public or if the concentration of wealth has negative effects on competition.[8] Since the Antitrust Division has limited resources, a staff of economists advises it about critical areas of the economy for official action. Consideration is also given to the desired goals of official action; criminal prosecution may succeed in punishing a past offense, but civil remedies may be more effective in securing compliance with the law.[9]

From 1890 to 1959 there were a total of 1,499 antitrust cases begun by the Antitrust Division; only 729 of them were criminal actions. A total of 486 of the 729 criminal cases were pursued to the imposition of a sanction. During this period of time, only 48 jail sentences were meted out, and many of them were suspended. Most of these jail terms which were actually served were for economic racketeering or for offenses by executives of small corporations.[10] In the period from 1940 to 1961 only twenty businessmen actually served jail sentences for antitrust violations; most of them served between 30 and 90 days in jail. This group of businessmen included officers of small, closely held corporations and relatively minor executives of large firms.[11] Only three different criminal *cases* between 1890 and 1970 led to the actual imprisonment of business executives.[12] When fines are levied on corporate executives, the amounts are often quite small; from 1950 to 1960, 256 executives were fined an average of $2,100 in antitrust cases.[13] In recent years there has been a decline in the proportion of all antitrust cases which are criminal actions as opposed to civil actions: 59 percent of the cases were criminal actions

[8]President's Commission, *Task Force Report*, p. 110.

[9]A.D. Neale, *The Antitrust Laws of the United States of America* (Cambridge, England: Cambridge University Press, 1970), pp. 373-400.

[10]John J. Flynn, "Criminal Sanction under State and Federal Antitrust Laws," *Texas Law Review*, 45 (October 1967), 1305.

[11]Alan M. Dershowitz, "Increasing Community Control over Corporate Crime: A Problem in the Law of Sanctions," *Yale Law Journal*, 71 (December 1961), 291.

[12]Ralph Nader and Mark Green, "Coddling the Corporations: Crime in the Suites," *The New Republic*, 166 (April 29, 1972), 18.

[13]Richard A. Whiting, "Antitrust and the Corporate Executive," *Virginia Law Review*, 47 (October 1961), 938.

in 1940-49, 48 percent were criminal cases in 1950-59, 31 percent were criminal cases in 1960-69, and only 9 percent were criminal cases in 1970.[14]

Many cases which the FTC might recommend to the Antitrust Division for criminal prosecution are instead handled administratively with sanctions available to the FTC, including cease-and-desist orders and injunctions. In 1965 the FTC dealt with thirty-three civil cases and recommended only ten for criminal prosecution; seven of the ten cases involved price-fixing. In 1966 twelve of the thirty-two cases it dealt with were recommended for criminal prosecution.[15] The FTC thus handles most cases without recommending criminal action, and the Antitrust Division prosecutes cases very selectively. Even in those rare cases which do lead to a criminal conviction, sentences are lenient.

In 1961 the most widely publicized prosecution of businessmen and corporations produced a number of convictions and jail sentences. A total of 45 executives from 29 different electrical equipment manufacturing companies were indicted for price-fixing and bid-rigging. Thirty-six executives and 21 companies pleaded guilty or *nolo contendere.* Fines of up to $12,500 were levied against the convicted executives. Twenty-eight executives received jail sentences ranging from 30 to 60 days. However, only seven of them actually served time in jail; the rest had their sentences suspended. Jail sentences were given to those executives who were most clearly responsible for setting company policy. Although these sentences were harsh by the usual standards for punishing business crimes, they were well below the statutory maximum and less than were recommended to the court by the Department of Justice.[16]

The electrical equipment price-fixing case also led to criminal fines for the corporations. Although these fines totaled $1.8 million, this amount was considerably less than the estimated cost of the crime to consumers.[17] The criminal fines were in the same proportion to the total wealth of the offending corporation as a $3 parking ticket for an individual with an annual income of $175,000.[18] A special IRS ruling allowed the

[14]Nader and Green, "Coddling the Corporations," p. 18.

[15]President's Commission, *Task Force Report,* p. 109.

[16]Anthony Lewis, "7 Electrical Officials Get Jail Terms in Trust Case," *The New York Times,* February 7, 1961, pp. 1, 26.

[17]Gilbert Geis, "White Collar Crime: The Heavy Electrical Equipment Antitrust Cases of 1961," in *Criminal Behavior Systems: A Typology,* ed. Marshall B. Clinard and Richard Quinney, (New York: Holt, Rinehart and Winston, Inc., 1967), p. 142.

[18]*Ibid.,* p. 142.

companies to deduct the fines on their income tax returns, so their financial losses were less than they appeared to be.

This dramatic case has been much written about, the publications including at least four full-length books. Little has been written on the topic of white collar crime without mentioning this extraordinary case. However, no other business executives were imprisoned in the years immediately after the case. The Department of Justice recommends imprisonment only when it is warranted by the nature of the act, the ability to pay a fine, and the age and health of the defendant. Such recommendations are rare; when they are made, the courts do not always accept them; and when a jail sentence is meted out, the length of the sentence almost never exceeds three months.

Selective prosecution and lenient sanctions were also the rule under the OPA from 1942 to 1947. Only 13,915 of 170,708 OPA enforcement proceedings which were closed by May 31, 1947, led to federal criminal prosecution. Only one of every ten or fifteen firms in the nation was punished for a rationing violation, although such violations were undoubtedly much more widespread.[19] Most of the cases which were prosecuted led to a conviction and a sentence. However, only 1,341 produced a prison sentence and a fine, and 1,629 others produced just a prison sentence. Another 5,312 led to a fine only, 3,318 produced probation or a suspended sentence, 1,500 cases were dropped, and 815 cases were lost by the government.[20] Thus only 8 percent of all of the closed proceedings led to federal criminal action, and only 21 percent of those cases which were prosecuted produced a prison sentence. Many of the fines meted out were less than the amount the offender had gained from his violation. Prison sentences which were actually served averaged less than six months. Clinard suggests that sentences were light because of public attitudes toward the offenses, the lack of a prior record for most offenders, and the circumstances of the crimes; however, most acts were clearly willful violations of the law and caused financial losses greater than those suffered in conventional crimes.[21]

Another area in which the federal government generally avoids the use of criminal sanctions is in the control of environmental pollution.[22]

[19]Marshall B. Clinard, *The Black Market: A Study of White Collar Crime* (Montclair, N.J.: Patterson Smith, 1952, 1969), pp. 33–35.

[20]*Ibid.*, p. 35.

[21]*Ibid.*, pp. 242–43.

[22]Michael K. Glenn, "The Crime of 'Pollution': The Role of Federal Water Pollution Control Sanctions," *The American Criminal Law Review*, 11 (Summer 1973), 835–82.

Under the recently reactivated 1899 Rivers and Harbors Act, pollution is a misdemeanor which is punishable by a jail sentence from 30 days to one year, and a fine of $500 to $2,500, or both. However, the position of the government has been to use the criminal law as a last resort and to try to negotiate compliance with the law. Civil injunctions are first used to achieve compliance; only if such measures fail will the threat of criminal action be made. Criminal charges are also initiated in cases of serious and repeated violations. In 1971-72 the Environmental Protection Agency referred 169 violations to the Department of Justice for prosecution. As of January 1, 1973, 39 of the cases had been refused for prosecution, 68 were under review or awaiting action, 19 had produced a *nolo contendere* plea and a fine, 22 had produced a finding of guilt and a fine, 6 cases had been dismissed, and 15 had other outcomes. In the 41 cases in which a fine was imposed, a total of $57,000 in fines was paid and $2,500 in fines was suspended. Almost half of the cases recommended for prosecution were for oil spills, and 15 were for other types of spills. During the same period of time, the Department of Justice itself began 63 additional criminal cases. As of January 1, 1973, 10 had led to a *nolo contendere* plea and a fine, 17 were pending, 22 had led to a guilty plea and a fine, 3 had led to trials in which the defendant was found guilty and fined, 5 had led to findings of guilt and probation, 2 were dismissed, and 4 had other outcomes. Up to the present, imprisonment has rarely been used for environmental law violators. Actions are usually brought against companies rather than individuals. Fines rarely exceed $1,000, which is often considerably less than it would cost the firm to comply with federal pollution regulations. The incentive to stop pollution is thus weak.[23]

However, in the last few years there have been some substantial fines levied against automobile manufacturers for falsification of data on pollution control standards. The EPA fined Ford Motor Company $7 million in 1973. In 1976 the State of California fined American Motors Corporation $4.2 million and banned the sale of certain AMC models in the state. An attempt to increase penalties for water pollution led to a 1972 amendment to the Federal Water Pollution Control Act. This amendment requires pollution permits which state all the requirements to which a discharger of waste is subject. Fines ranging from $10,000 to $50,000 and prison sentences ranging from six months to two years may be imposed for making false statements in the permit, for failure to

[23]*Ibid.*

notify the government of spills of dangerous substances, or for violation of permit requirements. The government can initiate criminal charges if the polluter fails to register for a permit, but such an action usually leads to quick registration and the subsequent dropping of charges. The criminal law is thus used as a prod to bring about compliance with the law, although stringent sanctions are available if needed.[24]

Leniency also exists in the prosecution and sentencing of embezzlers and employee thieves. Looking at data from 1933-44, Hall found that few embezzlers—possibly 1 percent—were prosecuted, and those who were convicted usually received probation or a suspended sentence. Judges often accepted restitution as a sanction, forgiving the offense if the victim would accept repayment of the loss. The sanction of restitution suggests that judges sometimes regard theft by an employee as a tort (civil wrong) to be settled between two private parties, rather than as a crime which involves the state and a defendant.[25]

A study of the prosecution of department store workers who had stolen from three different employers found that only 17 percent of a total of 1,681 cases led to prosecution.[26] The company's usual reaction was the immediate dismissal of the worker; only eight of those who were caught were retained at their jobs. Of those who were tried in court, 96 percent pleaded guilty and 99 percent were convicted. The high conviction rate resulted from selective prosecution; a criminal sanction was sought only when evidence of the crime was clear-cut and when a large loss had been sustained. In only twelve of the 256 convictions was a prison sentence imposed and served; in nine of those cases, the term was six months or less. Those who actually served prison sentences constituted only 5 percent of all who were convicted, and only 0.3 percent of all employee thieves detected by the three department stores. Thus, 95 percent of the sanctions were nominal—small fines (an average of $72), suspended sentences with probation (an average of seventeen months on probation), or restitution (an average of $637 to be repaid).

Criminal prosecution of business offenders is usually a last resort, one which is turned to if the offender refuses to comply with public or private attempts to undo the harm which results from his crime. Even when

---

[24]*Ibid.*

[25]Jerome Hall, *Theft, Law and Society*, 2nd ed. (Indianapolis: The Bobbs-Merrill Company, Inc., 1935, 1952), p. 311.

[26]Gerald D. Robin, "The Corporate and Judicial Disposition of Employee Thieves," *Wisconsin Law Review*, 3 (Summer 1967), 685–702.

there is a conviction in a criminal court, imprisonment is rare and fines do not usually exceed the profits from the crime. Business crime is thus dealt with much more leniently than traditional offenses which cost the public much less.

Reasons for Leniency toward Business Offenders

A variety of reasons exists for the lenient treatment accorded business offenders by the criminal justice system. In a sense, the leniency toward such offenders is overdetermined: any of the conditions which leads to leniency might by itself be sufficient to ensure the absence of harsh sanctions.

One reason for leniency is the absence of an influential and well-organized public demand for the prosecution and punishment of business offenders. The public might resist harsh sanctions for "respectable" businessmen, but it does not condone the actions of businessmen who violate the law. Rather, people feel powerless and unable to combat the powerful and wealthy corporations which influence the direction of legislation and law enforcement in this country. The public is not so much permissive toward business crime as it is resigned to it. As a result, little effective pressure is brought to bear on those who make the law or have the power to prosecute business offenders. With little to gain from the prosecution of white collar criminals and with the favor of business-men to lose, prosecutors usually avoid such cases and focus on conventional crimes.

Another reason for leniency toward business offenders is the infrequent reporting of their offenses to those who initiate prosecution. Victimization surveys since 1965 demonstrate that much conventional crime is never reported to the police. People do not report crimes because they think the police will not catch the offender or get their property back, they fear reprisals, they do not wish to be bothered by reporting the crime and testifying in court, or they know the offender personally and do not wish to cause him trouble. However, there is little solid information on the reporting and nonreporting of business crime. Because of the popular image of the police as "crime-fighters" who deal with conventional crime, business crime is probably not reported to the police very often because victims do not feel that the police handle that kind of offense. Also, because of the complicated nature of many business crimes and the offender's attempt to keep victims ignorant of their own victimization, many who suffer from a business crime remain unaware of it. Such crimes cannot be reported either to the police or to an interviewer in a victimization survey. One study of 76 victims of repair fraud found that only one-fourth of them reported the crime to someone with the authority to initiate action against the offender.[27] Thirty-nine percent of the victims felt that a complaint to the police would do no good and 10 percent felt that their victimization was not a matter for the authorities. Those who did report the fraud hoped that such action would protect others from exploitation. Few of those who reported the crime hoped to get their money back or see the offender punished.

Not only are few complaints of business crimes made to the police by the public, but employers whose workers have committed crimes against the company also fail to report many crimes to the police. Sometimes they report the crime to the insurance company in order to be repaid for their losses, but the insurance company rarely reports the offense to law enforcement authorities. We saw in the study of department store thieves that prosecution occurred in only 17 percent of the offenses which were discovered. Employers preferred to avoid the criminal justice system for a number of reasons. They thought that prosecution would create negative publicity for the company. Bringing the power and resources of the firm to bear against a lone offender would create a public image of vindictiveness and oppression, making the company look like a bully. Employers also thought that prosecution would harm the company because potential investors, customers, and employees would question the judgment of the company which had hired such an untrustworthy employee. Prosecution might also focus public attention on the fact that not all company workers are honest, leading potential customers and employees to avoid the company rather than risk dealing with another dishonest worker. Companies which require public confidence, such as banks, are especially sensitive to such considerations. Prosecution might also lead to the discovery of other illegal operations within the company or to the conclusion that lax internal security provided the opportunity for the crime. Prosecution is also avoided because it is time-consuming and expensive. Investigation and litigation may cost a company more than was lost in the original theft, and such costs are not usually covered by insurance and will not be paid for by restitution. In the study of

[27]Jack Horn, "Economic Crime: Portrait of an Arrogant Crook," *Psychology Today,* 9 (April 1976), 76, 79.

department store thievery, about three-fourths of the money which was stolen was recovered. Seventy-six percent of the workers made full restitution; 14 percent made some; and 10 percent made none. All who admitted guilt made at least some reparation; repayment was more common in crimes which involved the theft of smaller sums of money and which involved workers with more responsibility within the company.[28]

Companies sometimes avoid prosecution of a worker for fear that it will adversely affect the morale of other workers, especially if it is easy to sympathize with the dismissed worker because of personal problems which led him to steal. Workers may react negatively to the company's treating a former fellow worker as a criminal, since their stereotypes of criminals do not usually include a hard-working employee. Companies are also reluctant to prosecute a long-time employee who served the company well. In the study of department store theft, workers who had been employed for short periods of time, who had a poor work record, and who were of low status within the firm were most apt to be prosecuted. There was no difference in the rate of prosecuting males and females, those who were single and those who were married, or those who stole alone and those who stole in collusion with others.[29]

This study also found that the most important factor distinguishing cases which were prosecuted from those which were not was the amount of money stolen. Only 19 percent of the thefts involving less than $100 were prosecuted, but 57 percent of those involving a loss of more than $100 were prosecuted. The average worker who was prosecuted had stolen $608; the average worker who was not prosecuted had stolen $194. When people who had stolen similar amounts of money were compared, lower-status workers were prosecuted more often than higher-status workers, and male employees were prosecuted more often than female employees. Of the 338 cases which one of the department stores did not prosecute, 58 percent were not pursued because of insufficient evidence to secure a conviction, 13 percent were not pursued because the amount involved was trivial, 7 percent were not followed up for personal and family considerations, 6 percent were dropped because the prosecutor recommended against prosecution, and the other 16 percent were not prosecuted for a variety of other reasons.

Forty-five percent of the cases which that store did prosecute involved a situation in which restitution had been made or in which full recovery

---

[28]Gerald D. Robin, "Employees as Offenders," *Journal of Research in Crime and Delinquency,* 6 (January 1969), 30.

[29]*Ibid.,* pp. 18–20; and Robin, "Corporate and Judicial Disposition," pp. 685–702.

of the loss had occurred; thus nearly half of the prosecutions were for punitive rather than for economic reasons. In the other 55 percent of the cases which were prosecuted, criminal action was brought so that losses could be recovered. Prosecution depended on the amount of money stolen, but irrespective of whether or not there had been recovery of the loss, thieves who stole more than $100 were usually prosecuted if the company felt it could secure a conviction. In the prosecution of employee thieves there is essentially a private system of justice, with store managers making the ultimate decision as to when a case will be reported to law enforcement agents for prosecution. Such decisions are based on a desire to recover losses and to seek retribution, as well as on a desire to avoid the financial and social costs of prosecution.[30]

Offenders in the business world rarely suffer punishment at the hands of the criminal justice system because their offenses are rarely brought to the attention of law enforcement officials. The "dark figure"—the amount of actual crime which is never officially recorded as crime—is probably greater for business crimes than for conventional crimes. Victimization surveys suggest that even rape, one of the least reported of all conventional offenses, may be reported to the police as often as one time in four. This is a higher likelihood of being reported than the proportion of employee thefts reported to law enforcement authorities by the three department stores—17 percent. Considering that many department store workers are of low social status and that low-status offenders were reported to law enforcement authorities more frequently than high-status ones, it is likely that business crimes which involve high-status personnel (e.g., price-fixing, stock fraud, and false advertising) will be reported even less often than theft by department store workers.

When a criminal charge is brought against a business offender, there are a number of other reasons for lenient treatment by the criminal justice system. One is the high degree of cultural homogeneity among the defendants, the legislators who pass laws regulating businessmen, and the judges who determine guilt and mete out sentences to violators of those laws. Because businessmen, lawmakers, and judges come from similar social backgrounds, are of similar age, have often been educated at the same universities, associate with the same people, and have similar outlooks on the world, it is not surprising that legislators and judges are unwilling to treat business offenders harshly. Common backgrounds

[30]Robin, "Corporate and Judicial Disposition," pp. 699–702.

are sometimes exploited; as one person said, "it is best to find the judge's friend or law partner to defend an antitrust client—which we have done."[31] The defendant in a business crime case appears in court as a well-dressed and well-mannered citizen; the judge sees him not as a "surly felon menacing the public safety, but [as] a fellow country-club member who in a moment of weakness strayed from the path and now knows it."[32] Lawmakers and judges see businessmen as "respectable" because they have rarely been convicted of crimes; however, they have rarely been convicted of crimes because they are regarded as respectable. In one case, a judge refused to punish a businessman who had intentionally evaded the payment of income taxes, saying, "I will not penalize a businessman trying to make a living when there are felons out on the street."[33] In another case, Judge Henry J. Friendly overruled a $100,000 punitive damage award against a corporation by a lower court, claiming that such a large award would set a bad precedent: "A sufficiently egregious error as to one product can end the business life of a concern that has wrought much good in the past and might otherwise have continued to do so in the future, with many innocent stockholders suffering extinction of their investments for a single management sin."[34] This case arose out of Richardson-Merrell's manufacture and distribution of MER/29, which was not its only error; about the same time, it was also marketing thalidomide, a drug which caused birth defects in the children born of mothers who had used it. Friendly's willingness to overlook the harmful consequences of corporate behavior because of the good the company had done is reminiscent of a statement by a lawyer for one of the defendants in the Manson family murders; he called for leniency for his client because she had only engaged in murder for a few hours of the many thousands of hours she had lived.[35]

Judges are reluctant to impose harsh sanctions on business offenders who have not been convicted before, but due to this reluctance, few of

---

[31]Cited in Mark J. Green, with Beverly C. Moore, Jr., and Bruce Wasserstein, *The Closed Enterprise System* (New York: Grossman Publishers, 1972), p. 168.

[32]William E. Blundell, "Equity Funding: 'I Did It for the Jollies,' " in *Swindled! Classic Business Frauds of the Seventies,* ed. Donald Moffitt, (Princeton, N.J.: Dow Jones Books, 1976), p. 80.

[33]Harvey Katz, "The White-Collar Criminal," *Washingtonian,* 5 (May 1970), 65.

[34]Cited in Christopher D. Stone, *Where the Law Ends* (New York: Harper & Row, Publishers, 1975), p. 56.

[35]Vincent Bugliosi with Curt Gentry, *Helter Skelter: The True Story of the Manson Murders* (New York: W. W. Norton & Company, Inc., 1974), p. 449.

those defendants who do appear in court will have prior records. A study of 132 defendants in the Detroit meatpacking industry who were accused of OPA violations found that only two of them had previously been convicted of crimes.[36] Probably about 10 percent of all OPA violators had prior criminal records.[37] Only 2 percent of the apprehended employee thieves in one Chicago department store had criminal records.[38] However, Sutherland found that 60 percent of the corporations he studied had previously been convicted of crimes and many of those could be called "habitual criminals" because they had been convicted four or more times.[39] A more recent study discovered that at least 46 of 320 corporations convicted of criminal violations during 1964-68 had previously been convicted of a crime.[40] Apparently, individuals rarely have records of criminal convictions, but corporations frequently do. Because modern corporations are large and complex organizations which often involve operations in many states or nations and which often contain many workers at different levels and in different jobs, referring to a corporation as a "criminal" when one of its employees violates a law is sometimes no more accurate than calling an entire state a criminal if one of its citizens violates a law.[41] However, corporate employees frequently act in the name of the corporation, whereas the citizens of a state do not. If a crime is committed in the name of the corporation or if it involves actions related to the corporation as a whole, the corporation may be regarded as a violator, as may the employees of that corporation who actually violate the law. Some business crimes such as embezzlement and tax evasion take place in a corporate context but do not involve the corporation as an offender.

The social and cultural homogeneity of business offenders and judges is not the only reason for leniency by the courts. The courts also sought to avoid making criminals of department store thieves who were prosecuted. Although most of these workers were "respectable" and had no prior criminal record, they were not equal to the judges in social status.

---

[36]Frank E. Hartung, "White-Collar Offenses in the Wholesale Meat Industry in Detroit," *American Journal of Sociology*, 56 (July 1950), 29.

[37]Clinard, *The Black Market*, p. 295.

[38]Robin, "Corporate and Judicial Disposition," p. 698.

[39]Edwin H. Sutherland, *White Collar Crime* (New York: Holt, Rinehart and Winston, 1949, 1961), p. 25.

[40]Green, Moore, and Wasserstein, *Closed Enterprise*, p. 169.

[41]Thomas I. Emerson, "Review of Sutherland, *White Collar Crime*," *Yale Law Journal*, 59 (February 1950), 581-85.

The judges probably felt that the loss of a job was sufficient punishment for their crimes. They may also have thought that rehabilitation as commonly understood would be meaningless for such working people. Historical trends toward the increased consideration of prior criminal records, likelihood of recidivism, personal background, and circumstances of the crime have affected the sentencing of all types of offenders, whether they have been convicted of conventional crimes or of business crimes. Business offenders are not generally seen by the courts as good candidates for rehabilitation; judges reason that "recidivism is unlikely," "violators are *not* hardened criminals," "defendants are victims of economic forces," and it is "not clear in corporate crimes that guilty ones are in court."[42] One sociologist supports these views by assuming that white collar offenders "do not need resocialization" because they "are not characterized by antisocial attitudes or criminal self-images"; he suggests that what is needed are "alterations in patterns of social organization" rather than "tampering with individual persons."[43]

Business offenders also avoid prosecution and conviction because of their political influence and financial resources. Over the years, federal response to business crime has been linked to the prestige of businessmen. When prestige is low, prosecutions are relatively frequent; when businessmen enjoy high prestige, prosecution is less common. Wealth also allows businessmen and corporations to escape prosecution and conviction. Recently a Texas oilman claimed that his enormous fortune had been the direct cause of his acquittal on wiretapping charges; he said that he had been able to hire the best legal talent and investigators to offset the efforts of the prosecution. His ability to spend well over $1 million on the case made it unnecessary for him to plead guilty and difficult for the prosecution to secure a conviction.[44] As businessman Daniel Drew once said: "Law is like a cobweb; it's made for flies and smaller kinds of insects, so to speak, but lets the big bumblebees break through. When technicalities of the law stood in my way, I have always been able to brush them aside easy as anything."[45] It might be added that not only is the larger

[42]Green, Moore, and Wasserstein, *Closed Enterprise,* p. 168.

[43]Don C. Gibbons, *Changing the Lawbreaker: The Treatment of Delinquents and Criminals* (Englewood Cliffs, N.J.: Prentice-Hall, Inc., 1965), pp. 270–72.

[44]Martin Waldron, "Hunt Says Oil Fortune Was the Key to Acquittal on Wiretapping Charges," *The New York Times,* September 28, 1975, p. 40.

[45]Cited in Frank Pearce, "Crime, Corporations, and the American Social Order," in *Politics and Deviance: Papers from the National Deviancy Conference,* ed. Ian Taylor and Laurie Taylor (Baltimore: Penguin Books, 1973), p. 22.

bumblebee able to get through the web more easily than the fly, but the bee's sting also causes more harm than the fly's buzzing.

Even before committing an offense, businessmen may seek legal advice as to how to minimize trouble with the law; this advice may be cited in a trial as evidence that the businessman sought to avoid violating the law. Businessmen who are defendants in criminal cases hire lawyers who are highly skilled in defending their clients. They argue that their clients' health, lack of prior convictions, or low likelihood of recidivism warrant an acquittal or a light sentence. They cite numerous precedents in which no punishment was meted out to businessmen who engaged in similar behavior. They also seek to limit the evidence which is presented in court so as to conceal other offenses. One lawyer who handles white collar crime cases says that "most white collar cases involve a pattern of conduct that may be more widespread and more horrendous than the specific crime or crimes charged in the indictment. The vexing problem is what will one open oneself to by way of cross-examination on collateral matters."[46]

Businessmen also exercise power through control and influence over the media. This leads to the underreporting of business crime and its effects, thus leaving the public uninformed. Businessmen own television and radio stations as well as newspapers, and they also have the power to withdraw advertising from the media in which they receive bad publicity. White collar crime is rarely covered in much detail in the media because the press, especially daily newspapers, is geared to a 24-hour cycle in reporting. Many business offenses take place over long periods of time and do not have the high drama of such traditional crimes as murder and rape. The diffuseness and complexity of business crime and the event-orientation of the media keep business crimes off the front pages and hidden in the financial pages. One lawyer who has defended businessmen against criminal charges disagrees with the idea that the media are controlled by businessmen. Indeed, he finds the media "annoying" if not positively harmful to his clients and maintains a rigid rule against commenting on any pending cases.[47]

The absence of media coverage of business crime is well-illustrated by press reaction to the 1961 electrical equipment price-fixing case. A

[46]Harris B. Steinberg, "The Defense of the White-Collar Accused," *American Criminal Law Quarterly*, 3 (Spring 1965), 132.

[47]*Ibid.*, pp. 133-34. Some defenders of business feel that the mass media pay excessive attention to business crime. For example, see Kevin Phillips, "Why Coverage of Business News Is Sensationalized," *TV Guide*, September 25-October 1, 1976, pp. A-5-A-6.

survey of newspapers which covered 15 percent of the U.S. market in papers found that on the day after the indicted corporations admitted guilt, only 16 percent of those papers featured the story on the first page and no paper gave the story more than a single column headline. Another 11 percent of the papers gave the story less than one column of print on an inside page; 43 percent gave the story less than half of a column on an inside page; and 30 percent of the papers made no reference to the story at all. Another survey of 30 newspapers which covered 20 percent of the papers sold in the country was done after the sentencing of the executives and the corporations. Even after the unprecedented sentencing of a number of executives to jail terms, 45 percent of the papers did not put the story on the front page. The stories usually mentioned the sentenced executives but often failed to mention the guilt of the convicted corporations. References to the individual executives were phrased in terms of crime and criminal convictions; references to the corporations were in more neutral terms such as suits and penalties. The press coverage of this case did little to harm the public image of the corporations or to diminish their sales; the convicted executives acted as convenient scapegoats in many instances.[48]

In addition to the wealth and influence of businessmen, the very nature of their crimes works in their favor. Judges often view their offenses as trivial or technical, as violations of the letter of the law but not of any clearly defined moral standards. The image of business crime is that it does not involve significant harm, a view which is often incorrect.[49] Judges may also feel that it is unfair to expect businessmen to obey vague laws, although laws are often quite unambiguous and offenders are often aware that they are breaking the law. The criminal justice system usually enters the picture only when there is clear intent to violate the law. Nevertheless, some judges prefer to view businessmen as having good intentions, even when there is evidence to the contrary. In the case in which Judge Friendly set aside the damages against the producers of MER/29, he said that he found no "deliberate disregard for human welfare" and could see only "negligence in policing subordinates."[50] He attributed the marketing of the dangerous drug to lack of proper

---

[48]"Notes and Comment: Corporate Crime," *Yale Law Journal,* 71 (December 1961), 288–89.

[49]See the section on "The Costs of Business Crime" in Chapter 1.

[50]Cited in Sanford J. Ungar, " 'Get Away with What You Can,' " in Heilbroner and others, *In the Name of Profit,* p. 125.

managerial controls and refused to hold the corporation criminally responsible, although there was evidence to support such charges.

It is often difficult to infer criminal intent from an act. The law in the commercial world is sometimes written and interpreted to require unlawful intent rather than a mere intent to engage in behavior which happens to violate a law.[51] Proof of intent and of involvement in a criminal act may require the use of written records which are difficult for investigators to acquire, or they may require the use of testimony by a co-conspirator which is often difficult to secure. Sometimes intent may be inferred from the actions of law-violators. For example, the "camouflage of fictitious names and conspiratorial codes" used in the 1961 electrical equipment price-fixing case strongly suggested intent to conceal violations of the law.[52] Another type of behavior which suggests intent to violate the law is that businessmen involved in bribery will sometimes write checks for an amount just under that which triggers an investigation by the IRS.[53]

Proving intent may involve a problem of locating responsibility for certain actions within the corporate hierarchy. Questions as to which individual is responsible for a particular corporate crime or how much a particular executive should be aware of within the firm are not easily answered. Executives may claim that their subordinates were given certain duties but then "took the law into their own hands"; subordinates may claim that they were explicitly or implicitly ordered to violate the law in order to reach certain goals. Top managers were not indicted in the 1961 price-fixing case because it could not be shown that they knew of the conspiracy. Probably instructions to subordinates to fix prices or at least to stabilize the market were issued, but no written traces of such instructions were found.

Yet another element of the criminal justice system which explains the leniency with which business offenders are treated is the existence of the *nolo contendere* plea. In entering this plea when charged with a criminal violation, the company or the businessman is stating that he does not dispute the charges. This plea is supposed to protect those who violate the law without malice, inadvertently, or technically.[54] The *nolo*

---

[51]"Consumer Protection: New Hope Following Failure of Civil and Criminal Remedies," *The Journal of Criminal Law and Criminology*, 66 (September 1975), 277–78.

[52]Geis, "White Collar Crime," p. 143.

[53]Mintz, "Colonial Heritage," p. 83.

[54]"Antitrust Criminal Sanctions," *Columbia Journal of Law and Social Problems*, 3 (1967), 153.

plea is the same as a guilty plea for purposes of criminal action. However, it offers a major advantage to corporate defendants, since it cannot be introduced as evidence of legal guilt in a civil action; a guilty plea or a finding of guilt could be used to support a suit for damages. As a result, corporate defendants who are clearly guilty can avoid financial repercussions by pleading *nolo contendere* in criminal court but contesting a civil suit. From 1890 to 1970, 73 percent of all convictions in antitrust cases were by pleas of *nolo contendere;* during the 1960s, about four-fifths of the convictions were by this means.[55]

In addition to avoiding a presumption in favor of civil damages by pleading *nolo contendere,* such defendants usually receive lighter sentences because they have helped the court avoid the time and inconvenience of a trial. The *nolo* plea also has less stigma attached to it than a guilty plea or a guilty finding by the court. However, before agreeing to such a plea, the Department of Justice requires the defendant to say either in open court or in public that his plea is the same as a guilty plea, to acknowledge that he may receive as long a sentence as if he had pleaded guilty, and to promise that he will not publicly say that he was innocent of the charge. Judges usually permit a *nolo* plea if the prosecutor agrees, but they have the discretion not to accept it. Prosecutors may oppose a *nolo* plea if the crime is serious in terms of its impact on the economy, the extensiveness of the criminal conspiracy, the flagrancy of the act, or the clearness of intent to violate the law; they may also oppose it if a treble damage suit would be adversely affected. Between 1959 and 1965, judges agreed to the Department of Justice's recommendations to accept a *nolo* plea in all cases; however, they also accepted 96 percent of the defendants' *nolo* pleas which the prosecutors opposed.[56] Thus *nolo* pleas will generally be accepted by judges whether or not a prosecutor favors the plea. However, in the 1961 price-fixing case, the judge rejected a number of *nolo* pleas by defendants and forced the case to trial. Many companies and individuals who do have *nolo* pleas accepted by the courts later violate their agreements by issuing press releases stating that they pleaded *nolo contendere* in order to avoid the expense and delay of a trial, thereby implying that they are not really guilty.

The general philosophy underlying laws which regulate business behavior explains some of the leniency accorded business offenders by the criminal justice system. Until the early twentieth century, the domi-

[55]Green, Moore, and Wasserstein, *Closed Enterprise,* p. 163; Nader and Green, "Coddling the Corporations," p. 18.

[56]President's Commission, *Task Force Report,* p. 112.

nant philosophy was *caveat emptor* (let the buyer beware); people were expected to protect themselves from dishonest businessmen. Along with *caveat emptor* went a *laisser-faire* or hands-off attitude by government toward businessmen. With the rise of industrialization and with the growth in the power of small businessmen and the general public, laws and regulations to protect private property and to maintain a free enterprise system were passed. Since the late nineteenth century, a new way to deal with business behavior has emerged. The view that corporations might be sensitive to fines and the loss of prestige led to new laws with criminal sanctions. Regulatory agencies were created and given discretion to ask the Department of Justice to prosecute cases in criminal court. These agencies were also armed with a plethora of sanctions short of criminal action: cease-and-desist orders, contempt citations, treble damage suits, and others.

The dominant philosophy of these laws and regulations was remedial rather than punitive. More specifically, the regulation of businessmen was an attempt to secure compliance with the law *before* imposing a criminal sanction, whereas sanctions for conventional criminals were applied first and *then* rehabilitation of the offender was attempted. Nevertheless, the laws regulating business often include criminal sanctions, even if violations are usually dealt with in administrative agencies and civil courts rather than in the criminal courts. The decision to use civil sanctions rather than criminal sanctions is a result of "nonjuridical considerations" which are considered elsewhere in this chapter. The wealth and influence of businessmen is one such consideration, as is suggested by Sutherland's finding that during one period only 27 percent of the federal actions against businesses under the Sherman Antitrust Act were criminal rather than civil actions while 71 percent of the actions against labor unions under the same law were criminal.[57]

In civil proceedings, business offenders are dealt with much as young offenders are treated in juvenile court. The trend away from the punishment of juveniles around the turn of the last century was part of a general trend toward more lenient treatment of all offenders. This particularly affected business offenders, because many of the laws regulating business were passed at this time. Business crime is similar to juvenile delinquency in that each receives special treatment which is designed to protect the accused. One defense lawyer carried this analogy to an

[57]Sutherland, *White Collar Crime*, p. 48.

extreme when he addressed a judge as follows: "I know I represent a corporation, and rather *a young corporation,* if Your Honor please, which I am afraid *lost its way.* It was organized to build a pipeline from Texas to New Jersey and got lost around Woodbridge, *sadly enough.*"[58] The desire to minimize social stigma through special treatment is made clear in a statement made by the assistant to the head of the Department of Justice's Antitrust Division in 1940:

> While civil penalties may be as severe in their financial effects as criminal penalties, yet they do not involve the stigma that attends indictment and conviction. Most of the defendants in antitrust cases are not criminals *in the usual sense.* There is no inherent reason why antitrust enforcement requires branding them as such.[59]

In both juvenile court and regulatory agencies, due process is less adhered to than in criminal court. This usually serves the interests of the accused in cases of juvenile delinquency and business crime, but decisions made without due process of law may reflect the moral judgments of administrators and unfairly define innocent individuals as criminals.

Business offenders are thus "segregated administratively" from conventional offenders in the United States.[60] The use of administrative rather than criminal sanctions is also widespread in Great Britain and Canada.[61] In Great Britain, criminal sanctions are rarely used to control restrictive trade practices. In Canada, there is criminal prosecution only in rare cases of obviously illegal behavior, although criminal sanctions are available for restrictive trade practices. Criminal sanctions have been employed to deal with economic crime in the Soviet Union. Some acts which are defined as crimes there are not crimes in the United States, Great Britain, or Canada, e.g., engaging in private enterprise or in middleman activities. In 1961 Krushchev initiated the use of the death penalty for "exceptionally serious economic crimes," offenses in which the state or the public rather than a private party was the victim. Capital punishment has been used in the Soviet Union for such crimes as

---

[58]Cited in Mintz, "Colonial Heritage," p. 103. Emphasis added here.

[59]Cited in Sutherland, *White Collar Crime,* p. 43. Emphasis added here.

[60]Edwin H. Sutherland, "White Collar Criminality," *American Sociological Review,* 5 (February 1940), 8.

[61]John C. Spencer, "White-Collar Crime," in *Criminology in Transition: Essays in Honor of Hermann Mannheim,* ed. T. Grygier, H. Jones, and John Spencer (London: Tavistock Publications, 1965), pp. 239-49.

bribery and bribe-taking, counterfeiting, speculation in foreign currency, and embezzlement of public property. In 1975, five Soviet citizens were sentenced to death and fifty-nine others were sentenced to prison for an agricultural swindle which cost the state about $12 million.[62] The introduction and use of the death penalty since 1961 is part of a trend toward harsher punishment for business crimes in the Soviet Union. Some have suggested that it was also a manifestation of anti-Semitism; others feel that although the punishment of business criminals may have been an outlet for anti-Semitism, it was probably not initially conceived for that purpose. Although 30 to 60 percent of those who have been executed were Jewish, less than 2 percent of the Soviet population is Jewish. A higher proportion of Russians who work in business and commerce are Jewish and many of them are in middle-level positions in which they are less insulated from prosecution and punishment than their superiors, but it still appears that Russian Jews have been executed well out of proportion to their numbers in the population.[63]

In the United States the regulatory agency exists as an alternative to the criminal justice system for controlling business crime. However, these agencies have been generally unsuccessful in preventing abuses. Sometimes regulated groups have coopted the agency; publicly available calendars of regulatory agencies indicate extensive meetings with members of the industries which they are regulating, but few meetings with representatives of the public interest.[64] In a number of cases, individuals in the industry being regulated were the impetus for the formation of the agency in the first place. Regulatory agencies formed between 1890 and 1914 were generally supported by the industries they were to regulate, because those industries sought predictability and stable profits.[65] It was not long before businessmen were playing a major role in the administration of those agencies, either through influence or through providing personnel to staff the agencies. Although the regulatory commissions rarely came under the total control of the

[62]"5 Aides Doomed in Soviet Fraud," *The New York Times,* December 28, 1975, p. 7.

[63]George Feifer, "Russia Shoots Its Business Crooks," *The New York Times Magazine,* May 2, 1965, pp. 32-33, 111-12; George L. Kline, "Economic Crime and Punishment," *Survey: A Journal of Soviet and East European Studies,* 57 (October 1965), 67-72; and John. N. Hazard, "Soviet Socialism and Embezzlement," *Washington Law Review and State Bar Journal,* 26 (November 1951), 318-19.

[64]"U.S. Regulators Confirm Meeting with Regulated," *The New York Times,* December 8, 1975, pp. 53, 55.

[65]Pearce, "Crime, Corporations," pp. 18-25.

industries they were regulating, the outcry from businessmen whenever there is discussion of "deregulating" their industry strongly suggests that the agencies are serving rather than controlling them.

Regulatory agencies are kept weak by having restricted budgets, lacking the power to subpoena the records of companies which are under investigation, and being forced to rely upon reports by the manufacturers of new products rather than being given the resources to conduct in-house tests of those products. For example, the Food and Drug Administration has a low budget for enforcement and investigative staff and cannot force companies to provide them with their records. The Federal Trade Commission also lacks the enforcement staff which would be necessary to prosecute all cases and must thus rely on voluntary compliance and informal negotiation. Because many of the regulatory agencies lack resources, they must prosecute cases selectively. Most agencies do not have a clear set of priorities for the selection of cases for prosecution; having such guidelines would maximize their efficiency in using their limited resources. Offensive behavior is not now deterred because the certainty of prosecution and conviction is low and the severity of sanctions is not great.

The effectiveness of regulatory agencies is also reduced by links between the regulated and the regulator. For example, the Securities and Exchange Commission revealed in 1975 that groups from the securities industry often paid travel and hotel expenses for SEC personnel.[66] The fact that many who work for regulatory agencies know that they will work in the industry they regulate after leaving the agency leads to caution in enforcing the law; it is better not to alienate a company which may be a future employer. Many who work for regulatory commissions come from the industries which they regulate. One study of nine federal regulatory agencies found that more than half of those who were appointed to the agencies during the 1970-75 period had worked for the industries they were regulating. Although such regulators have expertise in the industry and may be more effective as a result, it is also likely that they will be less energetic in the enforcement of regulations because they are sympathetic with and have personal contacts with those in the industry.[67]

Because regulatory commissioners are political appointees and because politicians may harm an industry through the appointment of

---

[66]"S.E.C. Discloses Sponsors of Trips," *The New York Times,* August 29, 1975, p. 35.

[67]David Burnham, "Duality of Appointments to U.S. Agencies Scored," *The New York Times,* November 7, 1975, p. 14.

strict regulators, corporations seek to influence the appointment process. One way to influence who is appointed to regulatory commissions, as well as to affect the general stance of politicians regarding government regulation of business, is through campaign contributions. One result of the Watergate scandal was the revelation of a large number of illegal political contributions by large corporations and wealthy businessmen. Robert Vesco attempted to make a $200,000 contribution to the Nixon campaign as a way to stop an SEC investigation of his fraudulent stock transactions. Although there is a long-standing law against corporation contributions to campaigns for federal office, corporations such as Gulf Oil Corporation, Minnesota Mining and Manufacturing Company, Phillips Petroleum Company, Northrop Corporation, American Airlines, and Braniff International Airway have all admitted to illegal contributions. They used employees or front organizations to funnel money to candidates or "laundered" money in foreign banks before returning it to the United States as campaign contributions. Such actions violated SEC regulations against falsification of reports to stockholders, since contributions were usually concealed in general "slush funds." Such concealment suggests that corporate executives knew they were violating the law; this is also suggested by the fact that contributions were sometimes made by passing a plain envelope containing cash to a political aide in a remote place.

Minimal punishments have been meted out for these violations of the law. Action has rarely been taken against the politicians who accepted the illegal contributions; they usually claimed that they did not know where the money came from or that they had not used the funds for personal purposes. Corporations have been fined in a number of cases. Gulf Oil Corporation was fined $5,000 after pleading guilty to making an illegal contribution. The Associated Milk Producers, Inc., was fined $35,000 for illegal contributions. Two officers of the milk cooperative were sentenced to four months in jail; however, the judge said that he was not trying to rehabilitate them or even to punish them, but was merely trying to deter other businessmen from similar behavior.[68] Most of the 21 business executives who pleaded guilty during 1973 and 1974 to making illegal contributions continued to preside over their companies and were not treated as pariahs by fellow businessmen; a few were living in semi-retirement by 1975 as a result of their illegal actions.

[68]Anthony Ripley, "2 Get Jail Terms in Milk Payoffs," *The New York Times,* November 2, 1974, pp. 1, 16.

Only two had been in jail, and these had served only a few months. Most had paid small fines of one or two thousand dollars. Few were contrite, feeling that they had been singled out from the many who had engaged in similar behavior. For the most part they retained their wealth and their power in the business world, as can be seen from the table on the following page.[69]

Due to the absence of citizen complaints in many business crimes, regulatory agencies themselves must take steps to gather information showing that a violation has occurred. Often it is difficult to follow the "trail of evidence"; even when it can be followed, it often fails to show knowing complicity by particular individuals.[70] The complexity and low visibility of many business crimes, the diffuse impact and lack of clear-cut harm in such cases, and the inability to subpoena material for investigation pose obstacles which regulatory agencies often cannot surmount.

Business crime is detected in various ways. Antitrust prosecutions by the Department of Justice result from civil investigations by the Department, from disaffected corporate employees or executives, from federal purchasing agencies which report uniform bids to the Department, and from competitors and customers who lodge complaints.[71] Other federal and state agencies receive some complaints from victims, but many victims remain unaware of their own victimization or realize it too late for meaningful enforcement. Informants are a common source used to detect income tax and customs violations. Another source of information leading to prosecution or administrative sanction is an investigation by the staff of the agency; these investigations often require the skills of accountants and lawyers, as well as other experts. One question which has arisen in this context is whether the fruits of such investigations should be available to private citizens or corporations for use in civil suits. Because the cost of the investigation is borne by taxpayers, it has been suggested that they should have access to such reports for their own purposes.[72]

In its efforts to control business crime, the government sometimes uses inspectors to seek out violations of the law and secure compliance

[69]Michael C. Jensen, "Watergate Donors Still Riding High," *The New York Times,* August 24, 1975, p. 7.

[70]Morton Mintz and Jerry S. Cohen, *America, Inc.: Who Owns and Operates the United States* (New York: The Dial Press, 1971), p. 272.

[71]President's Commission, *Task Force Report,* p. 111.

[72]Herbert Edelhertz, *The Nature, Impact and Prosecution of White Collar Crime* (Washington, D.C.: U.S. Government Printing Office, 1970), pp. 33–35.

CONVICTED CONTRIBUTORS

Company	Name	Fine/Prison	Current Status
American Ship Building	George M. Steinbrenner 3d	$15,000	Still chairman at $50,000/yr.
	John H. Melcher Jr.	$2,500	Discharged. Practicing law in Cleveland.
Ashland Oil	Orin E. Atkins*	$1,000	Still chairman at $314,000/yr.
Associated Milk Producers	Harold S. Nelson	4 months prison $10,000	Resigned. Now in commodities exports.
	David L. Parr	4 months prison $10,000	Resigned.
	Stuart H. Russell	2 years prison**	Resigned. Now in private law practice.
Braniff International	Harding L. Lawrence	$1,000	Still chairman at $335,000/yr.
Carnation	H. Everett Olson	$1,000	Still chairman at $212,500/yr.
Diamond International	Ray Dubrowin	$1,000	Still V.P. for public affairs.
Goodyear Tire & Rubber	Russell DeYoung	$1,000	Still chairman of 2 committees at $306,000/yr. Also collecting pension of $144,000/yr.
Gulf Oil	Claude C. Wild Jr.	$1,000	Consultant in Washington, D.C.
HMS Electric	Charles N. Huseman	$1,000	Still president.
LBC&W Inc.	William G. Lyles Sr.	$2,000	Still chairman.
Lehigh Valley Cooperative Farmers	Richard L. Allison	Suspended Fine of $1,000	Discharged.
3M	Harry Heltzer	$500	Retired as chairman, but does special projects at $100,000/yr.
Northrop	Thomas V. Jones	$5,000	Still chief executive at $286,000/yr.
	James Allen	$1,000	Retired as V.P. with pension est. at $36,000/yr.
Phillips Petroleum	William W. Keeler	$1,000	Retired with pension est. at $201,742/yr.
Ratrie, Robbins & Schweitzer	Harry Ratrie	1 month probation	Still president
	Augustus Robbins 3d	1 month probation	Still Exec. V.P.
Time Oil	Raymond Abendroth	$2,000	Still president.

*Pleaded no contest   **Under appeal

with regulations. Inspectors are often overworked and must select targets for investigation and prosecution. They have significant discretion and can either seek compliance informally or recommend that legal sanctions be used. For example, inspectors who work for the United States Dairy Association to inspect meatpacking plants receive little guidance as to what action to take when faced with certain violations; instead they operate under the bureaucratic myth that all regulations are to be enforced. Were this actually the case, many plants would be closed. Although the proportion of actual violations leading to formal action cannot be determined for the meatpacking industry, one study estimates that less than 1 percent of all health and safety violations found by factory inspectors lead to formal action.[73] The competitive nature of the meatpacking industry provides an incentive for packers to cut costs by adulterating meats through excessive watering or by violating sanitary rules in the plant. Packers pay inspectors for overtime work, so that inspectors may gain financially by not alienating the packers. Packers also give inspectors gifts, favors, and work clothes. Because inspectors are not closely supervised by their superiors, they are easily influenced in the performance of their duties by those whom they are regulating.

Meatpacking plant inspectors distinguish gratuities from bribes, viewing gratuities as having no effect on their professional judgment. It is a felony for inspectors to accept anything of value from a packer, but the packer commits a felony only if he gives something to the inspector with an intent to influence him in the performance of his official duties. In the few cases in which the USDA has taken action, it has been much harsher on inspectors who take bribes than on packers who give them. Bribery of inspectors is a problem faced by many government regulatory agencies, e.g., there have been bribes offered to IRS collection officers to induce them to provide additional time to pay taxes owed rather than seizing assets to pay the taxes. Those seeking to influence inspectors may even devise ways to influence those who refuse to take a bribe. In one case involving an FDA inspector, a company under investigation deposited $10,000 in a secret bank account in the inspector's name. Although the opening of the account was unknown to the inspector, it made it impossible for him to cite the company for violations without subjecting himself to a charge of taking a bribe.[74]

One of the few systematic studies made of inspectors was an examina-

[73]Mintz and Cohen, *America, Inc.*, p. 280.

[74]John G. Fuller, *200,000,000 Guinea Pigs: New Dangers in Everyday Foods, Drugs, and Cosmetics* (New York: G. P. Putnam's Sons, 1972), p. 300.

tion of the enforcement of the 1961 British Factory Laws.[75] These laws were passed to make sure that the legitimate goals of a company were not pursued at the expense of its workers' safety, health, or welfare. Available criminal sanctions were rarely used, although a study of 663 reports found about 3,800 violations of the law by a total of 290 firms. Each firm had at least two reported violations during the four-and-half year period which was studied; one firm had 94 recorded violations. Most of the violations in the reports were not trivial. Three of every four were discovered during routine factory inspections; others arose from visits to the factory to check on complaints by employees. No formal action was taken in 5.5 percent of the recorded cases. Firms were notified of the matter requiring attention in 74.5 percent of the cases. In another 11.9 percent of the cases, firms received letters telling them that a matter urgently needed attention, although the letters did not mention the possibility of formal legal action. In 0.3 percent of the cases, there was a threat to issue a "certificate of unsuitability." In 4.5 percent of the cases, the possibility of legal action was mentioned, but there was no direct threat against the company if it failed to comply. In only 1.8 percent of the reported violations was there a direct threat of prosecution of the company. An additional 1.5 percent of the cases were actually prosecuted. Decisions to prosecute formally resulted from industrial accidents which were caused by operating machinery. In all of these cases, the violators pleaded guilty and paid fines which averaged ten pounds.

The British factory inspectors do not see themselves as part of an industrial police force which is concerned with the apprehension and punishment of offenders; rather they see themselves as government agents whose responsibility is to secure compliance with safety standards. They are concerned with the objectives of the legislation and choose the most appropriate means to reach them. Their approach is not punitive but is geared toward creating pressure for conformity to the law; an examination of state job safety practices in the United States also found a strong emphasis on voluntary compliance with regulations rather than with the enforcement of the law.[76] British factory inspectors took into

---

[75]W. G. Carson, "Some Sociological Aspects of Strict Liability and the Enforcement of Factory Legislation," *Modern Law Review*, 33 (July 1970), 396–412; and W. G. Carson, "White-Collar Crime and the Enforcement of Factory Legislation," *The British Journal of Criminology*, 10 (October 1970), 383–98.

[76]Joseph A. Page and Mary-Win O'Brien, *Bitter Wages* (New York: Grossman Publishers, 1973).

account such factors as the development of new machinery and new information on health hazards, trying to understand the social context of violations rather than simply to mete out punishment to violators. They felt that the firms violated the law but did not violate a "traditional part of our culture."[77] They employed a concept of "moral fault" to determine whether or not to take formal action against a violator. Reports of violations were used to determine if a company had been reluctant to comply with regulations in the past and to predict its likely response to informal action in the present. Severe sanctions might be recommended if prior reports showed a poor attitude toward legal obligations; in part, this attitude was assessed by the speed with which a firm complied with the law.[78]

This chapter has shown that the criminal justice system treats business offenders with leniency. Prosecution is uncommon, conviction is rare, and harsh sentences almost nonexistent. At most, a businessman or corporation is fined; few individuals are imprisoned and those who are serve very short sentences. Many reasons exist for this leniency. The wealth and prestige of businessmen, their influence over the media, the trend toward more lenient punishment for all offenders, the complexity and invisibility of many business crimes, the existence of regulatory agencies and inspectors who seek compliance with the law rather than punishment of violators all help explain why the criminal justice system rarely deals harshly with businessmen. This failure to punish business offenders may encourage "feelings of mistrust, lower community morality, and general social disorganization" in the general population.[79] Discriminatory justice may also provide lower-class and working-class individuals with justifications for their own violation of the law, and it may provide political radicals with a desire to replace a corrupt system in which equal justice is little more than a spoken ideal.

[77]Carson, "White-Collar Crime," p. 397.

[78]*Ibid.*, pp. 393–94.

[79]Richard D. Knudten, *Crime in a Complex Society: An Introduction to Criminology* (Homewood, Ill.: The Dorsey Press, 1970), p. 214.

six

Reducing Crime
in the
Business World

Many solutions to the problem of business crime have been recommended, but whether any of them can be implemented in the contemporary United States without basic changes in the social structure is debatable. Previous chapters have shown that business crime is closely linked to the society's dominant norms and values and to its social institutions. Even a major realignment of norms and values and a major reform of the social institutions might change the nature of business crime rather than eliminate it, for socialist and communist nations have their own problems with economic crime. However, certain social reforms seem to hold some promise for reducing business crime in the United States, even if they do not eliminate the problem altogether.

The Creation of a Countervailing Force

In recent years businessmen have grown defensive about their behavior, claiming that "profit" has become a "dirty word" and that "[i]t is impossible to conduct business in the U.S. today without breaking the law."[1] One reason for this defensiveness is the emergence of an increasingly strong consumer movement, a movement which is viewed with hostility

[1] Cited in Louis Finkelstein, "The Businessman's Moral Failure," *Fortune*, 58 (September 1958), 116.

by many businessmen. However, many of these critics of the consumer movement also admit that they have responded to consumer pressure, since only by doing so could they maintain and increase their profits. The further organization and education of consumers thus might reduce business crime to even lower levels by making businessmen more responsive to public pressure.

Consumer pressure has generally been the result of private efforts. Legislative efforts to create an effective consumer protection agency to act as an ombudsman for the public have been largely unsuccessful. Such an agency could become an advocate for consumers as well as an educative tool. The Consumer Product Safety Commission is a federal agency which has existed since 1973, but it is understaffed and slow-moving and has been the object of efforts to eliminate it. There have been congressional efforts to create an Agency for Consumer Advocacy which would appeal federal administrative and court decisions which are seen as harmful to consumer interests, would publish consumer complaints, and would conduct tests of products. Opposition has so far thwarted the development of such an ombudsman organization.

Existing consumer protection agencies could be made more effective if they were consolidated or shared information. Currently, it is difficult to show criminal intent in fraud cases unless a systematic pattern of abuse can be demonstrated through recurring complaints against the same firms or individuals; sharing of information among existing consumer agencies would facilitate the development of such cases for prosecution. Agencies could also be organized to handle complaints more quickly and to provide feedback for complainants on the outcome of cases. Another reform might be to expand the powers of certain agencies; for example, in 1975 the Federal Trade Commission was given power to bring certain cases to civil court and to seek remedies for consumers, thus providing it with sanctions beyond the cease-and-desist order.

A number of reforms might alleviate certain abuses of consumers. The holder in due course might be forced to accept greater liability for sales by merchants whose contracts they purchase, creating an informal pressure by the holder in due course on businessmen with whom he deals; efforts in this direction were made in 1975. Another change which has been recommended is a mandatory replacement or refund system under which losses to consumers from dishonest dealings with merchants would be spread over all taxpayers; such a system would require a regular audit to control dishonesty. Yet another possibility is the creation of private programs for mediation and arbitration. Mediation would allow for the resolution of merchant-customer disputes by a third party which would negotiate a compromise solution to a problem, and arbitration would allow for adjudication of a dispute through fact-finding efforts by a third party.[2]

One reform which would serve to educate consumers is the annual publication of a report on business crimes which could be presented in a press conference, much as the FBI's annual crime report is delivered. Such a report could provide details of administrative, civil, and criminal sanctions against business offenders. Although the press might not be responsive to such a report in the same way that it is to the FBI's Uniform Crime Reports, the press has given increased attention to business crime in recent years.

One sanction which could be employed to inform the public of business crimes would be to require companies convicted of breaking the law to use their own resources to pay for public advertisements about their own wrongdoing. Forcing a firm which has been convicted of false advertising to tell the public that it had deceived them would make the public more wary of that company's advertisements in the future. Most advertising is not criminally deceptive, but when it is, the offending party should be required to say so. Such "positive repentance"[3] could counter the public image of corporate infallibility which many companies seek to foster. The fact that corporations try to conceal employee theft and embezzlement from the public suggests that they are concerned with the effects of negative publicity. Thus a policy of requiring negative publicity when sanctions are administered might deter businessmen from violating the law. This technique has been used by the Food and Drug Administration, which has required drug companies found guilty of false and deceptive advertising to retract claims they have made by sending letters to physicians. This practice of having a company mail a "corrective letter" is used only in cases of a "major untruth." A 1967 study by the FDA found that no physician, group of physicians, or medical publications favored corrective letters. An alternative policy might be to make such letters publicly available through periodic press releases.[4]

[2]Mary Gardiner Jones and Barry B. Boyer, "Improving the Quality of Justice in the Marketplace," *George Washington Law Review*, 40 (March 1972), 364-80.

[3]Gilbert Geis, "Deterring Corporate Crime," in Ralph Nader and Mark J. Green, *Corporate Power in America* (New York: The Viking Press, Inc., 1973), p. 193.

[4]Morton Mintz, "Drugs: Deceptive Advertising," in *Hot War on the Consumer,* ed. David Sanford (New York: Pitman Publishing Corporation, 1969), pp. 93-94.

Adverse publicity for offensive behavior might lead to a consumer boycott of a particular company or at least to some decrease in its sales. However, it would probably be difficult to persuade the public to change its buying habits in any major way. There would be difficulties in informing all consumers of violations, and many consumers might remain unaware of their own victimization. Also, consumers might not know how to apply pressure to a company or might be unable to apply such pressure; for example, would price-fixing in the steel industry lead to a boycott of all car manufacturers? There is also a question as to how vulnerable to consumer pressure a large corporation would be; that would depend in large part on the position of the company in the marketplace. Adverse publicity would have to attract public attention, be simple enough to understand, and make clear what an appropriate consumer response would be.[5] The material examined in Chapter 2 suggests that there is an untapped source of public indignation about business crime which might be stimulated and organized through such efforts as adverse publicity.

Another possible way to reduce business crime is to reconceptualize the role of the corporation in American society. Since corporations are licensed by the state and are granted certain legal rights, they presumably have corresponding legal obligations. Treating corporations as "agencies of the state," which is the way in which they were once conceived, might produce a change in corporate behavior by holding them more accountable to the public.[6] Indeed, a variety of "corporate constituencies" might be defined so that corporate decision-makers would consider not only the interests of their stockholders but also the interests of their employees, union leaders, suppliers, consumers, and the public at large.[7] Public accountability has often been interpreted by businessmen and corporations as a need to tell the public how well they are treating the American public. Even when confronted with evidence of corporate wrongdoing, companies direct their attention to public relations rather than self-examination. One direct reaction to stories of corporate payoffs

[5]Brent Fisse, "The Use of Publicity as a Criminal Sanction against Business Corporations," *Melbourne University Law Review*, 8 (1971), 107-50.

[6]David P. Riley, "Taming GM . . . and Ford, Union Carbide, U.S. Steel, Dow Chemical . . ." in *With Justice for Some*, ed. Bruce Wasserstein and Mark J. Green (Boston: Beacon Press, 1970), p. 215.

[7]Arthur Selwyn Miller, "Business Morality: Some Unanswered (and Perhaps Unanswerable) Questions," *The Annals of the American Academy of Political and Social Science*, 363 (January 1966), 97-98.

and illegal campaign contributions was the presentation at a National Association of Manufacturers meeting of a multiple media show designed to explain free enterprise and the evils of government regulation of business.[8]

One way to increase corporate accountability is shareholder democracy, a system under which stockholders exercise real control over the corporation through elections, rather than having their votes effectively controlled by corporate directors. Other possible reforms which have been suggested to increase corporate accountability include federal incorporation laws which require the disclosure of certain information on corporate activities, public representatives on boards of directors, public availability of corporate income tax returns, and involuntary "social bankruptcy" for persistent violators of the law.[9] A special public directorship has been suggested for firms in areas of great social concern in which market and legal forces fail to keep industry in line with the public interest; this type of directorship would be used where there is a "demonstrated delinquency situation" and a generic industry problem which is not amenable to legal sanction.[10]

Legal reform might also create incentives for the public to take an interest in corporate behavior. Better reporting of business violations would provide more complete information about the extent and cost of such offenses. Incentives to employees to "blow the whistle" on violations by their employers might foster greater allegiance to societal obligations than to corporate policies. Rewards for the reporting of violations might create a "watchdog" public which would exercise informal control over businessmen. For example, the Rivers and Harbors Act of 1899 makes it possible for individuals who supply information leading to a criminal conviction to receive half of the fines paid by the offender. Laws which allow for rewards or which permit multiple damage suits create an incentive for the public to become involved in the control of business crime. Unless people are adequately compensated for their losses, for the cost of a lawyer to handle their case, and for the inconvenience of enforcing their legal rights, they will avoid involvement with the legal system.

[8]Steven Rattner, "Failure to Communicate Is Laid to Business at N. A. M. Parley," *The New York Times,* December 6, 1975, p. 40.

[9]Riley, "Taming GM," pp. 219-37.

[10]Christopher D. Stone, *Where the Law Ends* (New York: Harper & Row, Publishers, 1975), pp. 174-83.

One way to involve greater numbers of people in the legal system is the class action suit, in which a number of individuals who have suffered damages at the hands of the same offender join together to sue on behalf of themselves and all other individuals who are similarly situated. The usefulness of the class action suit has been curtailed by a recent court decision concerning the need to inform all parties to such suits about the proposed litigation and by another court decision concerning eligibility to bring class action suits in federal courts. Although there have been legislative efforts to expand the use of the class action suit, these efforts have been unsuccessful to date. Class action suits are potentially valuable tools for consumer education and for effective legal pressure on business offenders.

Reforming the Criminal Justice System

Some critics argue that business crime cannot be effectively reduced through increased use of the criminal sanction.[11] Ogren attributes this to the "natural limits" of the criminal justice system.[12] He claims that the lack of resources available for investigation and prosecution, the lack of public support for criminal sanctions, the ponderousness of the criminal justice system, the complexity of cases, the fact that most offenders would be dealt with as first offenders even if they had actually engaged in the behavior over a period of time, and the minimal deterrent effect of a few convictions all indicate that the criminal justice system is a poor way to deal with business offenses. He does concede that prosecution might have a symbolic impact or an educative effect on the public. A similar position was taken by the President's Commission on Law Enforcement and Administration of Justice in 1967. The Commission claims that the use of criminal sanctions in antitrust cases is uneconomical and ineffective. It also states that the increased use of the criminal sanction would dilute its impact. The Commission recommends the use

---

[11]See Robert W. Ogren, "The Ineffectiveness of the Criminal Sanction in Fraud and Corruption Cases: Losing the Battle against White-Collar Crime" *The American Criminal Law Review*, 11 (Summer 1973), 959–88; William N. Leonard and Marvin Glenn Weber, "Automakers and Dealers: A Study of Criminogenic Market Forces," *Law and Society Review*, 4 (February 1970), 410; and The President's Commission on Law Enforcement and Administration of Justice, *Task Force Report: Crime and Its Impact—An Assessment* (Washington, D.C.: U.S. Government Printing Office, 1967), pp. 104–6.

[12]Ogren, "Ineffectiveness," p. 960.

of alternatives to the criminal sanction, such as the withholding system which has reduced tax evasion; criminal sanctions should be used only as a last resort. The Commission also states that although imprisonment may deter business offenders, it will not rehabilitate them.[13] Although rehabilitation in prison does not seem to work for any criminal offenders, increased knowledge of business crimes might suggest effective programs for the reform of white collar offenders. The fact that most such offenders are neither hungry nor deprived when they engage in their crimes suggests that they may be more in need of rehabilitation than many conventional criminals.

Those who feel that the criminal justice system *has not* been effective in dealing with business crime imply that it *cannot* be effective. However, there is little evidence that there has ever been a real effort to control business crime through criminal sanctions. Material presented in Chapter 2 suggests that public support for harsher sanctions probably exists. More appropriations for investigation and prosecution might increase the deterrent effect of the criminal law. This would also circumvent the problem of many business offenders having no criminal record even though they have engaged in crime over a period of time; with more prosecutions, more offenders would have prior records when they are brought into court on new charges. There is little reason to think that the increased use of criminal sanctions against businessmen would reduce the impact of such penalties, as the President's Commission suggests; certainly this argument is not applied to conventional offenders. Whether rehabilitation of business offenders is possible cannot be determined at this time, since there have been few if any efforts to create programs for the few who have been incarcerated. Increased incarceration of such offenders might reform them by isolating them from justifications for their behavior and by demonstrating to them that their behavior is socially condemned, possibly breaking down their rationalization that their offenses were only technical violations of an arbitrarily designed law which lacked popular support. However, rehabilitation is only one of the functions of the criminal law.

A primary function of the criminal law is retribution, a function which is clearly not served by the law's treatment of business offenders today. As a justification for punishment, retribution theory proposes not only vengeance and repayment for the social harm which results

---

[13]President's Commission, *Task Force Report*, p. 104.

from crime, but also the idea that only the guilty should be punished and that they should be punished in proportion to the seriousness of their crimes. The general public feels that certain business offenses are more serious than some conventional crimes. The actual costs of business crimes exceed those of conventional crimes. Nevertheless, the law is rarely enforced against business offenders.

Another justification for punishment is deterrence. Specific deterrence is the prevention of future crimes by an offender because of his punishment for a given crime; general deterrence is the prevention of crimes by other potential offenders because they fear punishment similar to that which is meted out to another offender. Businessmen are not apt to be deterred by the threat of punishment if they are rarely detected committing an offense, if they are infrequently convicted, or if they are punished in a lenient manner.

Since bureaucracies are characterized by rational decision-making, it may be assumed that individuals in large corporations carefully plan their actions and execute them with possible consequences in mind. Such actions are usually instrumental (directed toward specific goals) rather than expressive (the result of personal needs); instrumental actions can be more easily deterred than expressive ones.[14] Most business offenders probably do not have a high commitment to their illegal behavior, i.e., they could easily give up their law-violating tactics. Low commitment to crime is also related to the ease with which behavior may be deterred by punishment. For deterrence to be effective, it is also necessary that there be a high certainty of punishment for a given act; obviously this is lacking for business crimes. If the certainty of sanction drops below a particular level, the law will no longer affect the risk-reward calculation of businessmen. When low certainty of punishment is combined with relatively lenient sanctions, deterrence is almost completely lacking. A small risk of a weak sanction is regarded as an acceptable risk by businessmen with something to gain by violating the law. Other characteristics of punishment which increase the deterrence of crime are also absent for business crime: promptness of sanctioning, public administration of the punishment, and application of the punishment with a proper judicial attitude.[15]

[14]William J. Chambliss, ed., *Crime and the Legal Process* (New York: McGraw-Hill Book Company, 1969), pp. 360-78.

[15]William C. Bailey, "Murder and Capital Punishment: Some Further Evidence," *American Journal of Orthopsychiatry*, 45 (July 1975), 671.

Middle- and upper-class individuals might be more sensitive to the status degradation which results from formal sanctions than would be true of those with less social status to lose. For such white collar offenders, criminal conviction and incarceration may symbolize social condemnation; this was suggested by the fact that electrical company executives who were imprisoned in the 1961 price-fixing case refused to have visitors at the prison because of the shame they felt.[16] Computer criminals also have a great fear of exposure of their crimes because of the embarrassment and loss of prestige among their peers.[17] Loss of reputation may be more important to white collar offenders than loss of money through a fine; therefore, adverse publicity which gives the names of individuals who have been convicted of business crimes might be an effective deterrent to such behavior in the future. The IRS follows a policy of recommending jail sentences for those convicted of income tax fraud, even if they are community leaders; it reasons that tax fraud is a rational act which can be deterred through the threat of a harsh sanction which costs the offender social status and prestige.

Because of the careful consideration given to profit maximization in the corporation, business crime might be deterred by harsher and more certain penalties. Jail sentences for responsible corporate officers, as well as increased fines for the firm, possibly based on corporate assets or on amounts gained through illegal activities, might force decision-makers to consider with greater care the risks of violating the law.

However, Christopher Stone questions the possibility of deterring business offenders by criminal sanctions. He suggests that because most criminal laws were originally devised to control individuals outside an organizational context and were then applied to organizations with little modification, many existing laws are inappropriate for corporate misbehavior. Corporations cannot simply be dealt with as individuals, nor can individuals operating within a corporate structure be treated in the same way as individuals outside such a context. Stone asserts that legal reform which takes into account the internal processes of organizations is needed in order to eliminate certain conduct, bring other conduct into line with the public interest, and distribute the costs of harm which cannot be prevented.[18] Although some corporate behavior can be con-

---

[16]Herbert A. Bloch and Gilbert Geis, *Man, Crime and Society,* 2nd ed. (New York: Random House, 1970), p. 310.

[17]Donn B. Parker, *Crime by Computer* (New York: Charles Scribner's Sons, 1976), pp. 48–69.

[18]Stone, *Where the Law Ends,* pp. 1–69.

trolled through fines, Stone claims that not all decisions are oriented toward profit maximization; e.g., a fine for the corporation may not deter criminal behavior by individual officers of the corporation if they personally gain prestige or income from violating the law.[19]

There is no convincing evidence of the deterrability of business crime. However, there is some reason to think that such behavior can be deterred. For instance, a 1941 study using a lie detector on 14,000 store clerks found that 76 percent had stolen cash or merchandise from the store; the test was done with the promise that no action would be taken on the basis of the results. A second test six months later, which clerks had previously been told might lead to dismissal or criminal charges, found that only 3 percent were still stealing from the store.[20] This experiment suggests that business crime might be deterred by increasing the risk of detection.

Lawyers who worked on the 1961 electrical equipment price-fixing case felt that the prosecution, conviction, and incarceration of the corporate executives in that case did in fact break up other price-fixing conspiracies. One convicted executive said that the jail sentences made people reexamine their moral values; apparently, white collar crime is "especially vulnerable to reform by threat of demeaning social sanctions."[21] One person who analyzed this case agreed with the executive, stating:

> No one in direct contact with the living reality of business conduct in the United States is unaware of the effect the imprisonment of seven high officials in the electrical machinery industry in 1960 had on conspiratorial price fixing in many areas of our economy; similar sentences in a few cases each decade would almost completely cleanse our economy of the cancer of collusive price fixing, and the mere threat of such sentences is itself the strongest available deterrent to such activity.[22]

Another effect of this case was that a number of corporations established preventive programs to reduce the chance of antitrust violations.[23] The

[19]*Ibid.*, pp. 30-69.

[20]J. P. McEvoy, "The Lie Detector Goes into Business," *Forbes,* January 15, 1941, pp. 16-17, 39-40.

[21]Gilbert Geis, "Criminal Penalties for Corporate Criminals," *Criminal Law Bulletin,* 8 (June 1972), 380.

[22]Gordon B. Spivack, "Antitrust Enforcement in the United States: A Primer," *Connecticut Bar Journal,* 37 (September 1963), 382.

[23]Richard A. Whiting, "Antitrust Enforcement and the Corporate Executive II," *Virginia Law Review,* 48 (January 1962), 3.

effectiveness and duration of these changes is unclear, but it is likely that the absence of additional jail sentences for businessmen in the years immediately after 1961 led to a return to previous business practices, if they had ever been altered at all.

Clinard feels that there was little or no deterrence of OPA violations because few offenders were actually sent to jail. When businessmen were dealt with by the criminal justice system, they usually received suspended sentences or probation; often they saw such sanctions as equivalent to acquittal. However, there was widespread fear of jail sentences among businessmen. Indeed, when substantial sentences were meted out, compliance with OPA regulations was more likely; such compliance apparently resulted from fear of sanctions, fear of injury to reputation, and respect for the law.[24] Although businessmen during the OPA era felt that prison sentences were the most effective sanctions available because they stigmatized offenders and curtailed their business activities, and although most businessmen had heard about the use of such sanctions, most businessmen felt that few offenders were actually punished harshly.[25]

One example of the deterrability of white collar crime is the low level of embezzlement in the United States Post Office.[26] Employees are apparently deterred by the efficient system of inspection and the policy of not accepting restitution in return for dropping criminal charges. Here a maximum likelihood of detection and prosecution creates a higher certainty of punishment than is the case for other white collar offenses. In the period from 1942 to 1951, 3,658 employees in U.S. Post Offices were charged with theft; 3,390 were found guilty, 48 not guilty, 70 *nolle prosequi*, 128 dismissed or quashed, 5 were disposed of in other ways, and for 17 there was no information on disposition. Thus over 90 percent of the defendants were convicted, a factor undoubtedly related to the low offense rate among postal employees. There is also a relatively low rate of embezzlement among bank employees which can probably be attributed to regular inspections and a high rate of prosecution and conviction. In the 1942–51 period, of the 2,766 defendants in bank embezzlement cases, 2,180 were found guilty, 78 not guilty, 216 pleaded *nolle prosequi*, 220 cases were dismissed, 10 were disposed of in other ways,

---

[24]Marshall B. Clinard, *The Black Market: A Study of White Collar Crime* (Montclair, N.J.: Patterson Smith, 1952, 1969), pp. 244–45.

[25]*Ibid.*, p. 244.

[26]Jerome Hall, *Theft, Law and Society*, 2nd ed. (Indianapolis: Bobbs-Merrill Company, Inc., 1935, 1952), pp. 327–30.

and for 62 there was no information on disposition. The legal require-ment that bank examiners transmit evidence of wrongdoing to local district attorneys and to the FBI produced a high certainty of punishment and a lower rate of employee theft than exists in businesses which are not subjected to such intensive investigations and such vigorous prosecu-tion policies.[27]

Tax evasion, a type of white collar crime which is sometimes but not always a business crime, may also be deterred. A study of a group of tax-payers with annual incomes over $10,000 looked at the effects of the threat of sanction and the effects of an appeal to the taxpayer's con-science and sense of patriotism. Subjects of higher social status were less affected by a statement of the moral reasons they should pay taxes than by the threat of a sanction, whereas lower-status individuals were less responsive to the sanction threat than to the conscience appeal. The authors of the study suggested:

> Less educated, working class people may be more prone to respond to con-science appeals because of greater piety or naïveté, or because of a con-viction that government action is needed for the solution of social problems. Alternatively, the better educated, upper class respondents may already have been exposed to such reasons for taxpaying and either accepted them . . . or be resistant to attitude change when it is implicitly urged on them. In regard to sanction, less educated, working class individuals may be inclined to discount the prospect of prosecution being directed against them, be less worried about the experience if it should occur, and be less likely to convert the fear of sanction into normative reasons for acquiescence.[28]

A realistic threat of a harsh sanction might deter income tax evasion be-cause it is a rational act. Low certainty of apprehension, the ability to negotiate a settlement with the IRS, and mild criminal sanctions would all reduce the likelihood that such behavior would be deterred.

Although increased punishment of business offenders would probably deter others from business crimes, the absence of many such sanctions up to now makes it difficult to know if business crime can be deterred in this way. Short of increased punishment, a number of legal reforms could also reduce business crime. Clarifying certain laws which regulate busi-

---

[27]*Ibid.*, pp. 327–32.

[28]Richard D. Schwartz and Sonya Orleans, "On Legal Sanctions," in *Society and the Legal Order*, ed. Richard D. Schwartz and Jerome H. Skolnick (New York: Basic Books, Inc., 1970), pp. 537–38.

ness and providing interpretations of how those laws will be applied would increase certainty and predictability for businessmen, making it possible for them to avoid behavior which is clearly in violation of the law. Creating laws which are specific, understandable, enforceable, inexpensive to administer, and uniformly applied would reduce rationalizations for business crime that laws are unfair or vague.

Another legal reform would be to eliminate the *nolo contendere* plea, which currently allows business offenders to escape the full impact of criminal sanctions and to avoid paying civil damages to victims. At the very least, the law could permit the introduction of the *nolo contendere* plea into civil proceedings as equivalent to a finding of guilt. Such a change might reduce plea bargaining and thus increase the number of trials for business crimes, since corporations and individuals would not plead *nolo contendere* if such a plea could be used to support a claim of civil damages against them. If *nolo contendere* pleas are retained, the law might at least require public notice when such pleas are made and accepted.

A related reform would be to reduce the use of plea bargaining and negotiation prior to trial. Tax fraud which is discovered by the IRS leads to prosecution only if evidence is sufficient to indicate guilt beyond a reasonable doubt and to secure a criminal conviction. However, the taxpayer's willingness to pay taxes which he owes is considered in the decision to prosecute; this is especially true if the taxes are paid prior to a full-scale investigation, about which the taxpayer is usually forewarned. Such opportunities to settle a case out of court probably reduce the deterrent effect of punishment.

Civil settlements which occur before criminal actions may impede the criminal prosecution of business offenders. If the results of criminal cases—whether a finding of guilt or a *nolo contendere* plea—were made available to plaintiffs in civil proceedings, they would have an incentive to await the outcome of criminal cases before pursuing their civil suits and they would be more willing to become involved in the criminal prosecution of business crimes, thus easing the prosecutor's task. This reform might also make the recovery of losses by victims more likely, reducing the disillusionment which often follows a criminal conviction in which victims are not compensated for their losses.

A distinction between the corporation as an entity and the employees of that corporation can impede both criminal and civil proceedings. Corporations can be dealt with as individuals which are subject to criminal and civil actions. However, they differ from individuals in that the intent which is often required to prove a criminal charge against an individual is absent in a corporate bureaucracy. Nevertheless, there are a number of conventional criminal offenses (e.g., statutory rape) which are strict liability crimes, i.e., intent does not have to be proved to secure a criminal conviction. Certain laws regulating business behavior might be revised to include a strict liability provision, thus obviating the need to show intent by the corporation or its officers. Some recent environmental pollution laws are of this variety, requiring evidence of pollution but not of intent to pollute. It is also a strict liability offense to fail to register a new stock issue with the SEC. The Food, Drug and Cosmetic Act contains a strict liability criterion which allows for certain sanctions even in the absence of personal knowledge of a crime or intent to violate the law.

The law regarding corporate crime might also be revised to focus responsibility for decision-making and policy implementation on certain corporate officers. They could be held responsible for those to whom they delegate certain duties, and they might be liable to criminal conviction if they are in a position to know of or are directly involved with criminal acts by their subordinates or if it is reasonable to impute such knowledge to them.[29] The law could require corporate officials to exercise care in controlling, preventing, and learning about wrongdoing within the firm. Examination of the firm's organizational chart would be one way to determine where to place responsibility for violations of the law.[30] An emphasis on tasks within the corporation would help to locate exactly which employee is responsible for specific illegal behavior.[31] Such changes might lead to better supervision of subordinates and more consideration of how company policy is formulated and implemented. Penalties could be enacted for failure to report a violation of which one is aware. A recent Supreme Court decision dealt with this issue of responsibility for business crime. This case involved a president of a supermarket chain who was found guilty in a lower court of causing food to be shipped in interstate commerce under unsanitary conditions. The Court held that "any corporate officer or agent who has the respon-

[29]Richard A. Whiting, "Antitrust and the Corporate Executive," *Virginia Law Review*, 47 (October 1961), 984.

[30]Robert H. Iseman, "The Criminal Responsibility of Corporate Officials for Pollution of the Environment," *Albany Law Review*, (1972), 94-95.

[31]Stone, *Where the Law Ends*, pp. 190-91.

sibility and authority to deal with matters within the coverage of the statute, must make an affirmative effort to seek out and remedy possible violations. Moreover, he must insure that effective measures are implemented so that violations will not occur."[32] The Court held that the corporate officer need not be a cause of the crime, participate in it, or have criminal intent; he need only have the responsibility and authority to bring about compliance with the law. In other words, he could be legally blameworthy even if he committed no wrongful action and had no intent to violate the law; he could not delegate his authority and thus escape the responsibility for corporate wrongdoing.

A policy of prosecuting both corporations and executives might be effective. Currently, many cases lead to a conviction of a corporation with a small fine as the penalty, but to the acquittal of all members of the corporation. By reducing the immunity of individuals to criminal sanctions through focusing responsibility, the deterrent effect of the law would be enhanced. Sanctions could alter the behavior of employees who would be most likely to suffer from a prison sentence or from personal disgrace. Punishing only the corporation usually means that fines will be levied; this usually causes a financial loss to stockholders (through reduced dividends) or to customers (through increased prices), rather than to corporate decision-makers. Punishment should fall on those who are responsible and on those whose future behavior will be affected by the prospect of punishment. As E. A. Ross wrote in 1907, "The directors of a company ought to be individually accountable for every case of misconduct of which the company receives the benefit, for every preventable deficiency or abuse that regularly goes on in the course of the business."[33] He also argued that officers of the corporation should be held blameless if they could prove that the inefficiency or disobedience of their subordinates caused the violation, but not if they merely claimed ignorance of their subordinates' behavior.

A policy of punishing individuals as well as their firms might employ not only such traditional sanctions as fines and jail sentences, but also innovative punishments designed for business offenders. For example, convicted offenders who are placed on probation by the court or paroled after a jail term might be prohibited from working for the same company

---

[32]This interpretation of the Supreme Court's decision in *United States v. Park* (421 U.S. 658 [1975]) appears in "Food and Drug Law—Standards of Corporate Liability," *Journal of Criminal Law and Criminology*, 66 (December 1975), 462–63.

[33]Edward Alsworth Ross, *Sin and Society: An Analysis of Latter-Day Iniquity* (Boston: Houghton Mifflin, 1907), p. 126.

or in the same field of endeavor for a period of time.[34] This would be no more burdensome than some of the probation and parole restrictions now imposed on conventional offenders.

Because of the cost and difficulty of investigating business crimes, many offenders are relatively immune to prosecution. Prosecutors may be unwilling to prosecute certain cases or may select cases for prosecution in a way which does not maximize deterrence. Making more resources available to regulatory agencies and to the Department of Justice would encourage the investigation and prosecution of more business crimes. In 1967 the combined annual budgets of the Federal Trade Commission and the Department of Justice's Antitrust Division were under $30 million, less than fifteen hours' worth of gross revenue for General Motors.[35] The Internal Revenue Service has too few investigators to audit all tax returns, although each additional agent who is hired yields about ten to twenty times his annual salary in additional tax revenue each year.

One necessary reform of regulatory agencies and prosecutors is a more target-oriented approach to prosecution. Focusing on cases with significant economic impact is necessary in the absence of sufficient resources. One effort along these lines is the IRS technique of simultaneously auditing all large companies in a given industry so as to establish whether certain patterns of abuse exist. One approach to a target-oriented policy might be the establishment of prosecutorial teams much like the strike forces which were pioneered by the Johnson administration to fight organized crime. Such strike forces could involve federal-state cooperation and sharing of resources and could employ experts to uncover violations in specific industries.

Another remedy which has been suggested for certain business crimes is the licensing of businessmen. Currently, relatively few businessmen are controlled through licensing, although some occupations such as stockbrokers and accountants are regulated in this manner. The licensing of door-to-door salesmen might make it easier to control certain abuses, although showing a license to a potential customer might create a false sense of security.[36] Some states have tried to prevent abuses by salesmen by allowing a "cooling off" period during which a customer who has

---

[34]Stone, *Where the Law Ends*, pp. 191-95; also see Leonard Orland, "Jail for Corporate Price Fixers?" *The New York Times*, December 12, 1976, Section 3, p. 16.

[35]Ralph Nader, "Business Crime," *The New Republic*, 157 (July 1, 1967), 8.

[36]Philip G. Schrag, *Counsel for the Deceived: Case Studies in Consumer Fraud* (New York: Pantheon Books, 1972), pp. 193-96.

purchased goods by contract can unilaterally rescind his agreement to buy a product within a given period of time. Two states license auto repair shops to prevent fraud; violators can be fined or temporarily suspended from doing business if they are found guilty of cheating on repairs or charges.[37] The licensing of occupations may be costly; an FTC study suggested that the regulation of television repairmen would drive up the cost of repairs by reducing the number of individuals repairing televisions.[38] Another area in which licensing has been attempted is in the area of pollution control. A 1972 law requires permits which specify all the requirements to which a waste discharger is subject; these permits provide a basis for enforcement actions.[39]

Some business crime might be curtailed through internal controls and audits. Accountants suggest that such measures can reduce embezzlement and employee theft. Division of responsibilities and closer supervision of workers who handle money and merchandise might reduce employee theft, as would greater plant security. Similar measures have been recommended to fight computer crime. The rotation of workers among jobs would also reduce the opportunities for theft within a company. Screening potential employees through background checks or lie-detector tests might weed out some potential thieves. The amount of business crime which could be eliminated through such controls is debatable. Accountants and consultants to corporations feel that closing the opportunities for theft will eliminate or greatly reduce the problem. Some sociologists such as Donald R. Cressey feel that such measures will be either ineffective or impractical, since they undermine the trust which is necessary for the smooth functioning of business.[40]

Businessmen sometimes propose that the solution to business crime is better self-regulation through a code of business ethics. However, businessmen have not been successful at self-regulation and have never developed a meaningful code of ethics which specifies appropriate behavior for particular situations. Businessmen more commonly try to

[37]Donald A. Randall and Arthur P. Glickman, *The Great American Auto Repair Robbery: A Report on a Ten-Billion Dollar National Swindle and What You Can Do About It* (New York: Charterhouse, 1972), p. 5.

[38]"Fraud Is Reported in TV Repair Work," *The New York Times,* January 13, 1975, p. 56.

[39]Michael K. Glenn, "The Crime of 'Pollution': The Role of Federal Water Pollution Criminal Sanctions," *The American Criminal Law Review,* 11 (Summer 1973), 881–82.

[40]Donald R. Cressey, *Other People's Money: A Study in the Social Psychology of Embezzlement* (Belmont, Calif.: Wadsworth Publishing Co., Inc., 1953, 1971), p. 153.

thwart government efforts at the regulation of business and react to the uncovering of business offenses with defensiveness rather than condemnation.

There is some question as to whether the creation of a strong countervailing force among the public and the reform of the criminal justice system can reduce business crime to any significant degree. Basic structural changes in the society and the economy may be required to reduce such crime, but there is no convincing evidence that any alternative social or economic system could keep business crime in the United States at a lower level. The effects of a stronger countervailing force and a more effective criminal justice system cannot be known until efforts are made to implement such reforms.

Index

Advertising
  bait-and-switch, 36, 59
  false, 7, 18, 22, 35-37, 51, 132
Agency for Consumer Advocacy, 131
Agriculture, Department of, 55
Airline industry, 35, 95
Air Transport Association, 95
Ambulance-chasing, 13
American Airlines, 124
American Motors Corporation, 107
Ansel, Hans Georg, 62
Anti-Semitism, 122
Antitrust violations, 4, 5, 7, 19, 22, 92, 103-5
Arbitration, 132
Arson, 2, 22, 44
Ashland Oil, Incorporated, 48
Associated Milk Producers, Incorporated, 124
Aubert, Vilhelm, 79
Audits, 146
Automobile industry, 5, 35, 53-54, 107
Automobile repairs, 4, 53, 90, 146
Automobile warranties, 53-54

Bait-and-switch technique, 36, 59
Bankruptcy fraud, 60-61
Bernhard, Prince of the Netherlands, 50
Black market, 25, 26, 55, 84

Blacks, 91
Bona fide purchaser, concept of, 63
Bonger, Willem, 60, 77-78, 83-84
Bongo, Albert Bernard, 48
Botulism poisoning, 5
Braniff International Airways, 124
Bribery, 3, 5, 35
  foreign, 48-51
  government regulation and, 54
  meatpacking industry, 55, 127
British Factory Laws (1961), 128
Bromberg, Walter, 74, 75
Burglary, 29, 30
Burroughs Corporation, 48
Business crime
  criminal justice system and (see Criminal justice system)
  defined, 13
  economic costs of, 2-8
  economy (see Economy)
  justifying, 86-99
  learning, 78-85
  mass media and, 1-2, 33, 116-17, 132
  psychological explanations of, 74-78
  public opinion and (see Public opinion on business crime)
  study of, 8-14
  victimless, 3
Buyer concentration, 51

Campaign contributions (*see* Political contributions)
Canada, 121
Caveat emptor (let the buyer beware), 120
Cease-and-desist orders, 103, 120, 131
Central Intelligence Agency (CIA), 6
Charitable donations, 42
Charity frauds, 58
Check forgery, 29, 30
Child-rearing practices, 77-78
Civil Aeronautics Board, 95
Civil law, 11
Class action suit, 135
Clinard, Marshall B., 66, 77, 84-85, 95-96, 106, 140
Competition, 4, 34-35, 41, 45-47, 51
Computers, 4, 62-64, 146
Construction industry, 54-55
Consumer fraud, 4, 8
Consumer movement, 130-33
Consumer Product Safety Commission, 131
Consumption-oriented economy, 34-41
Contempt citations, 120
Copyrights, 47
Cornfeld, Bernard, 56
Corporations
    bribery by, 48-51
    campaign contributions, 3, 5
    control of information within, 70
    false advertising, 35
    goals of, 41-43
    rational decision-making, 69
    reconceptualization of role of, 133-34
    structure of, 64-70
Corrective letters, 132
Credit, 41, 59-62
Cressey, Donald R., 39, 40, 59, 72-73, 87, 146
Crime statistics, 2
Criminal justice system, 100-129
    antitrust violations, 103-5
    embezzlement, 101, 102, 108
    employee theft, 108, 110-12
    environmental pollution, 106-8
    fines, 100, 101, 103-9, 138, 144
    jail sentences, 101, 102, 104-9, 138-40
    leniency toward business offenders, reasons for, 109-29
    nolo contendere plea, 105, 107, 118-19, 142
    prosecution and sentencing of business offenders, 100-109

Criminal justice system (cont.)
    reforming, 135-47
    regulatory agencies, 122-25, 127
Criminaloids, 8, 17, 79
Criminal sanctions, 135-36, 138
Cyclamates, 34

Dale car, 36
de Angelis, Tony, 60
Death penalty, 121-22
Debt payments, default on, 41, 60
Decision-making, rational, 69, 137
Demand
    growth rate of, 52
    price elasticity of, 52
Deterrence of crime, 137-41
Differential association theory, 77, 83-85
Dinitz, Simon, 83, 84
Distribution, 34
Drew, Daniel, 115
Drug importation, 44

Economic costs of business crime, 2-8
Economy, 34-41
    competition and profit, 44-51
    consumption-oriented, 34-41
    corporate structure, 64-70
    credit, 59-62
    market structure, 51-56
    trust, violation of, 56-59
Electrical equipment price-fixing conspiracy (1961), 10, 18, 52-53, 81-83, 91-92, 95, 105-6, 116-19, 138, 139
Embezzlement, 2, 4, 7
    causes of, 37-40, 74-76
    characteristics of embezzlers, 38-40, 73
    employee, 6, 13, 30-32, 59
    group, 75, 76
    justification for, 87-89
    prosecution and sentencing, 101, 102, 108, 140
    tension-reduction theory, 74-76
    (*see also* Employee theft)
Employee theft, 6, 13, 67-68, 146
    justification for, 88-89
    prosecution and sentencing, 108
    studies of public opinion toward, 27-30
England, Ralph W., Jr., 84
Entry barriers, 51, 52
Environmental pollution, 106-8, 143, 146
Environmental Protection Agency, 35, 107

Equity Funding Corporation of America
fraud, 46, 57, 65, 70, 81
Erdman, Paul, 99
Espionage, industrial, 47-48, 51
Ethics, code of, 146
Extortion, political, 13
Exxon Corporation, 48, 49

Fair trade laws, 5
False advertising, 7, 18, 22, 35-37, 51, 132
Federal Bureau of Investigation (FBI), 2
Federal Trade Commission (FTC), 50,
61, 103-5, 123, 131, 145
Federal Water Pollution Control Act
of 1972, 107
Fee-splitting, 13
Fines, 100, 101, 103-9, 138, 144
Food, Drug and Cosmetic Act of 1906,
23, 143
Food and Drug Administration (FDA),
45, 69, 123, 132
Food industry, 1, 23, 24
Ford, Gerald R., 95
Ford, Henry, II, 43
Ford Motor Company, 107
Foreign markets, 48-50
Free enterprise, 41, 93, 94-95, 98
Friendly, Henry J., 113, 117
Fringe benefits, 42
Full disclosure, rule of, 50
Fund-raising, 58

Gallup polls, 23, 24
Gambling, 37, 38
Gasoline dealers, 95-96
General Accounting Office, 5
General Electric Company, 42-43, 65
General Motors Corporation, 145
Gibbons, Don C., 22, 32
Goodman, Walter, 81
Government regulations, 54, 93-96, 120,
122-25, 127
Grain industry, 7-8, 55-56
Great Britain, 21
Grocery labeling, 4, 36
Group embezzlement, 75, 76
Guilt, 76
Gulf Oil Corporation, 48, 49, 124

Harris polls, 22
Hartung, Frank E., 26-27
Health hazards, 5, 22

Holder in due course, 61-62, 131
Home repairs, sale of, 36
Honolulu, landlords in, 96-97
Horning, Donald N. M., 76

Incorporation laws, 134
Industrial espionage, 47-48, 51
Industrial sabotage, 7
Innovation, 47
Insurance, 6
Interest rates, 22, 41
Internal Revenue Service (IRS), 50, 141,
142, 145
International market, 56
Investors Overseas Services, 12, 56, 57
Irving, Clifford, 57

Jail sentences, 101, 102, 104-9, 138-40
Japan, 67
Jaspan, Norman, 59, 68
Jones, Alfred Winslow, 28
Judges, 108, 112-13, 117
Justice, Department of, 92, 103-5, 125, 145
Justification of business crime, 86-99
Juvenile delinquency, 86, 120-21

Khrushchev, Nikita, 121
Knapp Commission Report of Police
Corruption, 54
Krueger, Ivar, 58
Kutschinsky, Berl, 29, 30

Labeling, 4, 36
Labor racketeering, 58
Laissez-faire, 120
Land, sale of, 35, 59
Landlords, 96-97
Lane, Robert E., 66, 84, 93-94
Law, ignorance of, 93
Legal system (*see* Criminal justice system)
Leonard, William N., 53
Licensing of businessmen, 145-46
Liebow, Elliot, 68
Living standards, embezzlement and,
37-39
Loan sharking, 44
Lockheed Aircraft Corporation, 48, 49, 50
Lottier, Stuart, 74-76

McDonnell Douglas Corporation, 48
Mannheim, Hermann, 73
Market structure, 51-56

Mass media, 1-2, 33, 116-17, 132
Meatpacking industry, 16, 26-27, 35, 55, 114, 127
Mediation, 132
Medical quackery, 13
MER/29, 45-46, 69, 113, 117
Merchant-customer relations, 90-91
Merck & Company, Incorporated, 48
Mills, C. Wright, 80
Minnesota Mining and Manufacturing Company, 124
Montgomery Ward, 6
Morris, Albert, 9
Muckraking tradition, 9

National Association of Manufacturers, 79, 134
Nettler, Gwynn, 40
Neutralization, techniques of, 86
Newman, Donald J., 23
Nolo contendere plea, 105, 107, 118-19, 142
Noncompetitive market situations, 4-5
Northrop Corporation, 49, 124

Office of Price Administration (OPA), violations of regulations, 10, 25-26, 30, 44, 55, 84-85, 96, 114, 140
Ogren, Robert W., 135
Omnipotence, fantasy of, 74
Organized crime, 44
Orutno, Rene Barrientos, 48
Overbilling, 51

Parker, Donn, 64
Parole, 144-45
Pasamanick, Benjamin, 21
Patents, 47
Payments, default on, 41, 60
Payoffs, 54, 55
Personality variables, 72, 77, 85
Pharmaceutical industry, 5, 45-46, 69, 113, 117
Pharmacists, prescription violations by, 44-45
Phillips Petroleum Company, 124
Plea bargaining, 142
Political contributions, 3, 5, 100, 124
Pollution, 106-8, 143, 146
Prescription violations, 44-45

President's Commission on Law Enforcement and Administration of Justice, 7, 135-36
Price-cutting, 47
Price elasticity of demand, 52
Price-fixing, 1, 47
electrical equipment conspiracy (1961), 10, 18, 52-53, 81-83, 91-92, 95, 105-6, 116-19, 138, 139
General Electric case (1950), 65
Pricing information, 36
Probation, 103, 144-45
Product differentiation, 51
Professionals, 14
Profits, 41-51, 52
Prosecution of business offenders, 100-109
Psychological explanations of business crime, 74-78
Public opinion on business crime, 7-8, 16-33, 109
comparative judgments, 22-23
employee embezzlement, 30-32
employee theft, 27-30
honesty of businessmen, 23, 24
moral attitudes, 21-22
OPA regulations, violations of, 25-26
socioeconomic status and, 24
studies of, 20-33

Radio repairs, 90
Rational decision-making, 69, 137
Recidivism, 115
Reckless, Walter C., 73, 83, 84
Record industry, 35
Red Fox, Chief, 57
Regulatory agencies, 122-25, 127
Rehabilitation of business offenders, 136
Rent control, 97
Repair fraud, 36, 53, 66, 88, 90, 110, 146
Research espionage, 7
Retribution theory, 136-37
Rettig, Salomon, 21
Richardson-Merrell Pharmaceutical Company, 45, 69, 113
Rigging bids on contracts, 52
"Rip-off mentality," 19
Rivers and Harbors Act of 1899, 107, 134
Ross, E. A., 8, 17, 144

Sabotage, industrial, 7
Scams, 61

Searle, G. D., & Company, 49
Securities and Exchange Commission (SEC), 5, 70, 123, 143
Securities industry, 4, 5, 18, 38, 62-63, 101, 102
Self-concept, 87, 88, 96
Self-regulation, 146
Seller concentration, 51
Sentencing of business offenders, 100-109
Severance pay, 42
Shareholder democracy, 134
Sharp, Frank W., 60
Sherman Antitrust Act of 1890, 103, 120
Shoe manufacturing, 44, 83, 93
Shoplifting, 6, 92
Short-weighting, 55
Socialization, 77-78, 85
Socioeconomic status, opinions on business crime and, 24
Soviet Union, 46, 67, 121-22
Specialization, 65
Sporkin, Stanley, 65
Stocks (*see* Securities industry)
Stone, Christopher, 69, 138-39
Strike forces, 145
Student attitudes toward business crimes, 20-21
Sutherland, Edwin H., 8-13, 16, 24, 35, 47, 72, 79, 83, 85, 114, 120
Swiss banks, 56, 99

Taft, Donald R., 84
Tanaka, Kakuei, 50
Tax evasion, 29, 30, 66-67, 97-99, 101-2, 136, 138, 141, 142
Tension-reduction theory, 74-76
Thalidomide, 113
Trade, restraint of (*see* Price-fixing)
Treble damage suits, 103, 120
Trust, violation of, 32, 56-59
Tying-in agreements, 55

Unemployment benefits, abuse of, 13
United Brands Company, 49
United States Dairy Association, 127
United States Post Office, 140

Veblen, Thorstein, 8
Vesco, Robert, 12, 56, 57, 124

Warranties, automobile, 53-54
Watch repairs, 90
Watergate scandal, 124
Weber, Marvin Glenn, 53
White collar crime (*see* Business crime)
White Collar Crime (Sutherland), 9
Withholding system, 136
Working conditions, health hazards and, 22

Zeitlin, Lawrence R., 68